Master

Key sk

and succe...   s

Mastering Negotiations

Key skills in ensuring profitable and successful negotiations

Eric Evans

THOROGOOD

Published by
Thorogood Ltd
12-18 Grosvenor Gardens
London SW1W 0DH
0171 824 8257

A catalogue record for this book is available from the British Library

ISBN 1 85418 057 6 (Trade edition)

ISBN 1 85418 195 5

Printed in Great Britain by Ashford Colour Press

The author

Eric Evans

Eric Evans is a very experienced seminar presenter and a widely published author on negotiating, selling and purchasing techniques. Prior to establishing his own consultancy practice, he was an executive consultant with Ernst & Young and Price Waterhouse.

A former Supplies and Commercial Manager with Dunlop, he was also a senior lecturer at the North West Regional Management Centre and is currently a visiting speaker at several universities. He has conducted numerous negotiating workshops, both publicly and in-house, for a wide variety of organisations, both in the UK and internationally.

Contents

Icons

Throughout the Masters in Management series of books you will see references and symbols in the margins. These are designed for ease of use and quick reference directing you quickly to key features of the text. The symbols used are:

We would encourage you to use this book as a workbook, writing notes and comments in the margin as they occur. In this way we hope that you will benefit from the practical guidance and advice which this book provides.

Alternative approaches to negotiation

Chapter 1

All too frequently we learn to negotiate through trial and error. We may stick to tried methods that worked once. We may make the same mistakes year after year. Individual experience may give you an adequate ability to negotiate, but it can never give you an insight into the wide range of possibilities that are available.

Nierenberg

This chapter puts negotiation into context as a business skill. It explores the way that most people learn negotiation skills, and suggests the flaws in this approach which need to be corrected if success is to be assured on a regular basis. It describes the key differences between win/win and other forms of negotiation.

What is there to master?

Man has been negotiating since Eve persuaded Adam to eat the apple. Since the time of the ancient Greeks, Romans and Babylonians; entrepreneurs, traders, businessmen and politicians have sought to resolve their differences by negotiating.

It has been said that in spite of the fact that man has split the atom, mastered the skills of transplant surgery and walked on the moon, the way we negotiate has changed very little since these ancient times. This is largely true, but does not do justice to the fact that there are scientific approaches to negotiation, tools and techniques for dealing with difficult situations, and lessons we can learn from experience. A body of knowledge has been captured and is available to be shared with those who have a thirst for understanding and improving their negotiation skills.

We start this book with the view that it is not only businessmen who negotiate. Those of us who say that we don't negotiate are missing the point that negotiations take place in any situation where one person is trying to persuade another. Every day we negotiate with our bosses, our subordinates, our peers and our colleagues, and then we go home and negotiate with our families and friends. We buy goods and services, from retailers and individuals, and even if we don't haggle, we are looking to persuade or influence the person we are dealing with. The same skills are used at work, at home and when we buy for ourselves, or when we try to sell ideas to others. Often the same mistakes are made. This book attempts to prevent these mistakes, to open up the subject of negotiation to detailed examination and to share the approaches that increase the probability of success.

So what is negotiation?

There are as many views on what negotiation is as there are people who negotiate. These views vary, and seem to point us in many different directions. Figure 1 overleaf gives some of the alternative definitions taken from discussions with professional negotiators, and some of these are worthy of further discussion.

Definitions of negotiation and the alternative directions they take us in

Figure 1

So which is it? It is perhaps easier to start by explaining what negotiation is **not**.

Argument?

Arguments frequently happen in a negotiation, but the question is should they? Negotiation is not the same as argument. Have you ever watched two people arguing? Apart from the obvious factors such as the existence of emotion, the absence of any 'real' listening, pre-occupation with a single point of view, the most striking thing is how, at the end of the argument, each person has convinced himself that he was right, without moving the other person one centimetre. Negotiation must involve persuasion. It is about moving somebody from their point of view, not about digging in. It must include an approach that is designed to encourage the other person to change their point of view, something which argument does not accomplish.

Discussion?

Nor is negotiation the same as discussion. You can discuss something such as sport, politics or religion for hours without ever reaching agreement. A discussion will often lack the emotion of an argument, but may be as ineffective in persuading people. Discussions can also be aimless – a way of simply passing the time or exploring alternative points of view. How often have you been involved in a discussion that ended without any firm conclusion? Negotiation has a purpose.

Compromise?

There is no doubt that compromise may be required at some point in a negotiation, but setting out with the intention of compromising is not good practice. Those who set off with the intention of compromising will usually send a strong signal to the other party that they are prepared to move, and this can be taken as a sign of weakness. Those in the habit of compromising will encourage their opponents to start out with an exaggerated posture. In reaching agreement, they may have been manipulated into accepting a deal that favours the other party. It is possible to reach agreement without compromise, and this idea will be developed as we go through this book.

Getting your own way?

This view of negotiation ignores the other party. Concentration on what you want out of the negotiation without taking into consideration the needs of your opponent is a recipe for conflict. Some argue that getting your own way is **what** you are there to do, the question is **how** you do it. There is logic in this approach, but it is still too narrow a view of negotiation. It suggests a predominantly self-centred approach which may work in the short term, but which will not sustain a good relationship.

Negotiation is, therefore...

It is possible to build a strong view of what negotiation should be. It is clearly a process that:

- Involves persuading people;
- Attempts to resolve differences;
- Has certain rules, conventions and norms;
- Impacts upon the relationships that people have with each other; and
- May be driven by logic, power, compromise, trading, emotion or a genuine problem solving approach.

What is more important than our perception of what negotiation is, however, is the perception that your 'opponent' has. If you believe that negotiation is about compromise, and you are negotiating with someone who sees it as a win/lose, then it is likely that this will work against you. As well as having a clear view of what you believe negotiation to be, you should have a clear view of how the other party views the process.

How we learn to negotiate

Key Learning Point

Few of us give a great deal of thought to what negotiation is. We have all negotiated since we were children, and unfortunately, through trial and error, we tend to reach our own particular approach to negotiation. Without a systematic consideration of alternatives, we have a chance of finding the best way to negotiate and the significant risk that we won't.

Even as adults, we rarely think about the process of negotiation. Figure 2 below shows a range of mental states we adopt whenever we are doing any activity. Research suggests that most of us negotiate in a state of 'Unconscious Competence'; we are competent because we are experienced, but just as we walk, talk, drive or drink, we negotiate without thinking.

Key Question

Negotiating 'States of Mind'

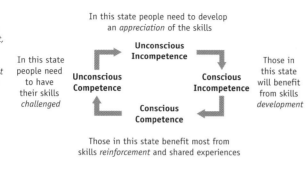

In this state, you do not possess the skills (incompetence) but are unaware of the fact that skills even exist (unconscious)

In this state people need to develop an *appreciation* of the skills

In this state you are, on the surface at least, competent, but you carry out the skill without even thinking about it. This can lead to complacency, mistakes and poor performance, and habit replaces conscious decision making

In this state people need to have their skills *challenged*

Unconscious Incompetence

Unconscious Competence

Conscious Incompetence

Conscious Competence

Those in this state will benefit from skills *development*

In this state you still do not possess the skills but at least are aware that the skills exist. This is arguably the healthiest state of mind if it encourages people to acquire the skills that are needed

Those in this state benefit most from skills *reinforcement* and shared experiences

In this state you possess the skills, but have to think carefully about what you are doing to put them into practice

Key Management Concept

Figure 2

The healthiest state to be is arguably, 'Conscious Incompetence'. In this state, there is a desire for improvement, as we strive to acquire better skills and techniques.

The rest of this chapter begins the process of increasing awareness of what negotiation is. The chapters that follow then focus on how to improve our skills and approach to negotiation.

Alternative approaches

If you ask people whether they believe negotiation should be win/win or win/lose, the overwhelming majority will tell you that is should be win/win.

Yet there are too many times when you come out of a negotiation feeling that you have lost, to believe that all negotiations are win/win.

It also has to be said that very frequently our words and actions do not match. What we say and what we do are often at odds with each other. We may believe in win/win, but we actually practice something which is much more competitive.

Compromise

There are also many misconceptions of win/win. Fisher and Ury in *Getting to Yes* (1) ask how two sisters with one orange should share it. Most people suggest splitting the orange in half. If one sister then eats the fruit from her half and throws away the peel, and the other throws away the fruit and bakes a cake using the peel, it becomes clear that there is a major difference between compromise and win/win. We shall explore this difference later in the text.

Win/perceived win

There *are* significant differences between what people say and what they do. In reality people who say they believe in win/win, often practice a form of win/perceived win. This involves winning, but making the opponent feel that he or she has won, often when they have no right to feel that way. Think about the last time that you were involved in a major personal purchase such as a house or a car. If the salesman or estate agent gives in too easily you feel cheated. He has to make you work hard so that you value whatever concession you get, however small. This is 'perceived win' and it plays a major role in many negotiations. Think about the things you can do to give someone the impression that they have secured a good deal.

Win/lose

Very few people believe that win/lose is the way to negotiate. There are times, however, when it may be appropriate. In one-off negotiations where one side is relying on power and has no need for a long-term relationship, win/lose negotiation will often take place. We will spend very little time talking about win/lose negotiation. It is not really negotiation but rather the crude application of power or coercion with no thought of the consequences. Where this book covers win/lose negotiation, it is to consider how to deal with an opponent who has a great deal of power in a situation where you do not.

Genuine win/win

In 1967 after the six day war in the Middle East, Israel had captured a large piece of Egyptian territory. Long negotiations ensued during which the American mediators suggested splitting the contested territory in half to resolve the problem. This compromise was unacceptable to both parties. As is often the case with compromise, it would have meant a lose/lose. Neither side would have met their objectives.

Eventually, the mediator asked the Egyptians why they wanted a piece of land that appeared to have little value. There were no oil or other mineral resources, nothing grew there, few people lived there. The Egyptians explained the profound political and social consequences of going home and explaining that they had given away land that had belonged to Egypt for thousands of years. When Israel was asked why they wanted the land they explained that they were worried about Egyptian tanks invading their land. The captured territory served as a buffer zone.

The agreement that was reached was that the territory be returned to Egypt but declared a de-militarised zone. Both sides won.

Many negotiations involve parties taking some form of posture and the negotiation takes place at this level. As Figure 3 shows, for a win/win to take place, the negotiation needs to be at the level of 'genuine objective'. This requires a conscious decision. Win/win does not just happen. It requires a positive decision by at least one party to get out of positional negotiation and search for a solution that will satisfy both sides' genuine objectives. This is often difficult to do.

Key Learning Point

Compromise versus win/win

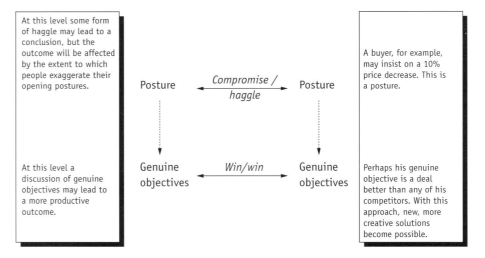

Figure 3

For many people win/win is an inappropriate term. The word 'win' introduces an air of competitiveness and needs to be eliminated. Some talk of integrative bargaining, the idea of two parties working together to 'make a bigger cake' rather than splitting the cake, others talk about 'principled negotiation'. Some talk about this form of negotiation being a genuine attempt at problem solving.

Which is it? It is all of these things. At times, it is an intensely competitive process, at other times it is a collaborative process. It is well to remember that at each of these ends of the spectrum there are different skills and behaviours required for success. What is appropriate in one type of negotiation may be totally inappropriate in the other.

From here we will replace terms such as win/win, win/lose, principled, integrative or distributive bargaining with the terms competitive and co-operative negotiation.

Key Learning Point

You always have a choice

If you were to observe an intensely competitive negotiation as a fly on the wall, what behaviours would you see and hear? Would these behaviours be similar or different to those you would see in an intensely co-operative negotiation?

The characteristics of competitive and co-operative negotiation

Key Question

Extreme forms of competitive negotiation contain extreme forms of behaviour. Similarly, extreme forms of co-operative bargaining will contain extreme forms of different behaviours. Imagine watching two negotiations, one intensely competitive and the other intensely co-operative. As an observer, you would see behaviour from the negotiators such as (overleaf):

Intensely competitive	Intensely co-operative
Play their cards close to their chests, and perhaps even mislead over their true position	Develop a degree of trust to the point where both sides can be open with each other
Exaggerate their demands so that they can appear to concede while giving nothing away	Treat the negotiation as a genuine problem solving exercise
Use strong emotive language which is often in the form of threats	Use positive emotions, for example, emphasising the benefits that a solution will bring to both sides
Argue strongly in favour of their demands and their positions, while ignoring the demands of the opponent	Listen to the needs of the other side and seek to address the concerns of both parties
Raise their voices as logic is replaced by emotion	Seek clarification of issues rather than re-buff them
Allow suspicion and hostility to determine courses of action	Replace suspicion and hostility with a desire to work towards common goals and objectives
Use tactics such as pressure, bluff, brinkmanship	Use tactics such as lateral thinking, re-framing problems to stress common features and objectives.

Action Checklist

It is difficult to understand how such competitive behaviour can be helpful in resolving differences of opinion and building commercial or trading relationships, but there are many competitive negotiations that exhibit some or all of these characteristics.

The key issue in competitive negotiations centres around the fact that each negotiator is trying to satisfy his own objectives, and if the opponent manages to satisfy his objectives then this is a bonus. Co-operative negotiations, on the other hand, involve each negotiator trying to resolve both sets of issues.

One American commentator talks about the amount of energy expended by two teams in a tug of war, each side counter-acting the other. This is like a competitive negotiation. Just imagine how much further the teams could move, he said, if they were both pulling in the same direction! This silly but easy to imagine analogy, sums up the difference between competitive and co-operative negotiation.

It is superfluous to ask which type of negotiation, competitive or co-operative, does most to build strong commercial relationships. Nor is it necessary to ask which type of negotiation produces antagonists and deep-seated resistance to change. Yet there are more competitive negotiations than co-operative negotiations. Before exploring what we can do to achieve a co-operative negotiation, it is worth looking at the reasons why there are so many competitive negotiations.

The drive towards competitive negotiations

Over the last 15 years of training and consulting experience, I have witnessed innumerable business simulations, and real negotiations that have resulted in competitive encounters when co-operative approaches have been possible. On consulting assignments where clients have asked my colleagues and I to assess the strengths of their negotiators, we have also found that a competitive approach, usually win/perceived win, is the most common style

There are a number of reasons why this happens:

Man is a competitive animal

There is no doubt that man is a competitive animal. 'Winning' is often translated into 'winning more than the opponent' even when a good outcome for both sides is possible and the opponent is not really an opponent. Although such 'competitive behaviour' does not drive everybody's negotiation style, there is no doubt that it is a major influencing factor for many of us.

Lack of trust

We are equally afflicted with a suspicious nature. Until a good relationship is built up we prefer to play our cards close to our chest. Even when we have built a relationship we often prefer to focus on the negative side of someone's personality and behaviour, rather than the positive side.

This is not to say that we should be naïve in trusting everyone, but simply to point out the consequences of failing to build good working relationships.

History

Once we have had a bad experience in a relationship with a customer or supplier or colleague, we tend to behave as though this negative behaviour will continue. There is an almost inevitable consequence of this fact. Once you treat someone as though they are not trustworthy, they tend to sense the way they are being treated and behave accordingly. This leads to an 'I told you so' situation. Such behaviours then turn into self-fulfilling prophecies as both sides lose trust and behave accordingly.

Perception of facts

It is often said that if negotiations were based on facts there would be less disagreement. Unfortunately this loses sight of the fact that there are usually different perceptions of the same facts. There is a very old joke about two shoe salesmen who go out to deepest Africa. One sends a fax back saying 'Wasting my time, no-one wears shoes'. The other sends a fax back saying 'Great news, no-one wears shoes'. The same facts, but two different perspectives.

You only have to stop for a minute and think about a buyer and a seller looking at a supplier's profit figures to see how this translates into business situations. Just how easy is it, for example, for a buyer and a seller to agree on a fair profit margin?

Self-centred negotiations

We also suffer from the fact that we often go into a negotiation looking to satisfy our own objectives without giving too much thought as to how we can give our opponent what he is looking for. If we are honest with ourselves, we would admit that there are times when we go into a negotiation without caring about what the opponent wants.

There is a sad inevitability about two negotiators, each looking to satisfy his own objectives without looking to satisfy the other party.

Learnt behaviours

We start to negotiate as children, and even at this early age, we start to learn and develop behaviours which will stay with us into our business and professional lives. Unfortunately, many of us learn competitive rather than co-operative skills. All parents experience a sadness when the innocence of childhood gives way to a more manipulative phase. We learn to be manipulative, scheming or Machiavellian through our own experiences and as we look to role models provided by television and the cinema.

None of this is intended to suggest that all negotiations should be co-operative. There are times when co-operative is not a valid approach and competitive negotiations are essential. In situations where you cannot trust the opponent, where the other party will not move towards a co-operative approach, where there is no need for an ongoing relationships should you really go for a win/win? All of these situations may lend themselves to a competitive approach to negotiation.

What is necessary is for each negotiator to make a deliberate decision at an early stage of a negotiation, rather than simply lapse into competitive negotiation.

Best Practice

You always have a choice. Negotiations can be competitive or co-operative. Rather than follow the knee-jerk reaction into a competitive negotiation, there is much to be said for making a *conscious* decision about whether it would be best to hold a competitive or co-operative negotiation. Many of us operate in a state of unconscious competence and do not make a conscious choice.

It helps to remember that starting a negotiation co-operatively brings more flexibility. If you start a negotiation in an intensely competitive style and it doesn't work, how easy is it to then become co-operative without losing your credibility and looking like you are on the retreat? Alternatively, you can always start a negotiation in a relatively co-operative stance and if this fails then move into a more competitive stance.

Later in this book there is a prescription for running co-operative negotiations and guidelines on how to move even difficult people towards a more co-operative stance.

Summary and concluding remarks

Key Learning Point

You always have a choice. The style of the negotiation is frequently dictated by short term circumstances, the history of the relationship and our innate personality and behaviours. It is better to decide on the type of relationship that you want with an individual and then consider the style of negotiation that will lead you in that direction.

The descriptions earlier in this chapter that highlight the characteristics of intensely competitive and co-operative negotiations leave no real choice in looking at the best basis for a business relationship, or a relationship with colleagues. Even though we rarely see such intensely competitive behaviour, most competitive negotiations exhibit some or all of these characteristics. We have a duty to try to develop sensible business relationships with our colleagues, customers and suppliers and this must mean looking at co-operative approaches.

Subsequent chapters of this book explore both co-operative and competitive approaches in more detail. The key theme is that co-operative is better but you must not ignore the fact that competitive may be appropriate.

The following chapters of this book will encourage you to think about your approach to negotiation. In particular they will seek to answer 12 key questions:

1. *In negotiation, is there a difference between 'win/win', compromise and 'win/perceived win'?*

2. *How does behaviour differ in these three types of negotiation?*

3. *What are the key things to do when planning for a negotiation, given a limited amount of time?*

4. *How does the truly successful negotiator differ from the average negotiator in the way he or she behaves?*

5. *How can you make sure that you are in control in all stages of a negotiation?*

6. *How do you persuade someone to do something as part of a negotiation?*

7. *If you reach an impasse in a negotiation, what can you do to make progress?*

8. *Why are some people difficult to negotiate with, and what can you do when dealing with them?*

9. *What are the benefits and drawbacks of negotiating in a team with colleagues, rather than on your own?*

10. *What are the most frequently made mistakes in negotiation?*

11. *What can you do to improve your negotiation skills?*

12. *How do you know when you have negotiated a good deal?*

Mastering the planning stage

Chapter 2

The will to win is nothing unless you have the will to prepare

Anonymous

The man who plans carefully before entering a negotiation, understands how to leverage his own strengths and those of his organisation. With careful plans, one can predict which alternatives for action offer greater opportunities. With superior execution, one can turn these greater opportunities into ultimate victory.

Adapted from *Sun Tzu – The Art of War*

This chapter sets out the actions that we should take in the planning stage of a negotiation. It draws on research that sets out how successful negotiators differ from average negotiators in their planning behaviour.

British Electronics: a case study

Activity

The following case study is based on a real negotiation that took place some years ago. The names and circumstances have been changed so that it is impossible to identify the real companies that were involved. You are invited to consider how you would plan for this negotiation. At the end of the chapter, the actual solution is revealed…

For the last seven or eight years British Electronics, a major international player in the field of computing and electronics, has been struggling hard to maintain its position as market leader in increasingly competitive times. Throughout this time a number of Far East competitors have come into the market with the benefits of lower labour and overhead costs.

To some extent the company has tried to mitigate the effects of its high cost-base by sourcing a number of major components and sub-assemblies from countries such as Korea and Taiwan. This has certainly helped to keep the costs down, and, it must be said, to keep the quality levels high.

The difficulties of sourcing from the Far East are only known to those who have had the pleasure of dealing with the problems of long supply chains, foreign currency transactions and the sheer administrative hassle of dealing with people who do not speak English well. It would have been so much worse if British Electronics hadn't managed to find a peach of a supplier in Kim Sun of Korea. They were a low cost, high profit supplier, with excellent quality, and the ability to respond quickly to customer needs.

Their performance on the wretched PC3 development project was typical. They had been a regular supplier of PC2 for about five years, and when PC3, the logical successor was first mooted, Kim Sun happily agreed to undertake the development work with British Electronics. They didn't actually have a written contract for this work, but both parties were happy to assume that the Koreans would be awarded the production contract, and that the development costs would be recovered in the overheads. The development work went very well and British Electronics were just about to award them a production contract when there was a subtle development.

The Swedish Government had issued an invitation to tender to British Electronics for a computer installation worth an immense amount of money. After putting together a first class proposal British Electronics, together with a Japanese conglomerate, were shortlisted. Then the Japanese firm played their trump card. They revealed that they were about to finalise the details of a new factory in Sweden. This would obviously bring much employment and prosperity to Sweden, and wouldn't do their bid for the Government contract any harm either.

British Electronics felt that there was overcapacity in the industry, and therefore to offer to build another factory would be counter-productive.

It was at this point that the Managing Director took a decisive step. It took the form of a memo to the Head of Purchasing. The salient points were:

'…obviously need to do something positive to secure the Swedish contract…I also feel it is time we sourced more components from Europe, with all the benefits this brings… I have found a Swedish supplier called Oblo… leading supplier of electronic components and products in Sweden… Their Managing Director is well known to me… you WILL source the new PC3 from Oblo… this is critical… it is also critical that you keep the cost of PC3 to a minimum… we cannot afford to burden our product costs… please tie up the loose ends on the contract as soon as possible'. *This is unequivocal! Kim Sun have quoted a price of £5.80 per piece, delivered UK, and including all development and tooling costs.*

British Electronics anticipate that their year 1 requirement will be 240,000 estimated to increase to 360,000 in year 2 and 480,000 in year 3. They must have the first 20,000 in eight weeks time, or the entire PC3 project may be in jeopardy.

The Sales Director from Oblo is about to call. Oblo are very successful, but are largely into Scandinavian markets at the moment, and have to buy many of their materials from abroad. Incidentally, their price is £7.60 delivered UK. This is a new product area for them, but there is no doubt that they are technically capable.

Assume that you are the Head of Purchasing for British Electronics.

1.   *How would you plan for the negotiation?*

2.   *What would your negotiation plan include?*

3.   *What information would you seek before negotiating?*

This case study will be referred to throughout the rest of this chapter.

What is there to plan?

It is difficult to conceive of a solicitor going into a court case without preparing, or a musician going into a concert without rehearsing. Yet many of us frequently go into a negotiation without adequate preparation.

Intuitively we know that it is important to prepare for a negotiation. The argument that the longer we prepare for a negotiation the better, sounds plausible. Some academics have put forward the view that for every hour spent negotiating, you need to spend between five and eight hours planning. Few practitioners, however, have the time available for this level of preparation.

Fortunately a key piece of research suggests that this is not necessary. Neil Rackham (2) conducted research aimed at understanding the difference between successful negotiators and average negotiators. This research found very little difference between the amount of time spent by average and successful negotiators when planning for negotiations. The major difference was *how* they spend their time.

Key Management Concept

Research by Rackham and others suggests that planning activities should focus on a number of key task and process issues.

Task issues

There are a number of basic issues that need to be covered in any negotiation. These task issues tend to be more closely related to the specific subject of the negotiation.

Task issues: information

It has been said that information is power. Nowhere is this more true than in negotiation.

It doesn't really matter what you are negotiating about, if you do not have enough information you can only *hope* to succeed, and this is just not good enough. The emphasis in professional buying in large organisations these days is to gain full information on supply markets, possible suppliers and products that are being purchased, including full cost breakdowns, details of supplier cash flow, liquidity and profitability, and market share. Similarly, salesmen are expected to know the buyer's volumes, purchasing policies, buying habits and details of his existing supply arrangements. The salesman is also expected to be fully aware of the competitors' prices, capacity and utilisation levels and their stock position. Without hard data on which to base a negotiation, the negotiator must work from assumptions, impressions and feelings. This would be amateurish.

Activity

Can you list the information requirements for the buyer from the British Electronics case study at the start of this chapter?

Clearly in looking at the case study there are a number of 'hard' and 'soft' information issues. The hard issues would include factors such as the supplier's capacity, capability, cost structure and any information on major contracts won and lost, the soft issues would include the messages passed between the two Managing Directors, and any information which exists on the Sales Director. This would include his interests, his negotiating style, his key business goals and objectives.

Psychologists have suggested that in preparing for negotiations we are often more conscious of our weaknesses and our opponent's strengths. This suggests a need to force our attention onto our own strengths and our opponent's possible weaknesses, while not ignoring their strengths and our weaknesses.

Completing the matrix shown below in figure 4 is usually helpful in providing that balance.

Strengths and weaknesses analysis

	Our position	**Their position**
Strengths	1. 2. 3. 4. 5. 6.	1. 2. 3.
Weaknesses	1. 2. 3.	1. 2. 3. 4. 5. 6.

Figure 4

In assessing the strengths and weaknesses in the buyer's position from the British Electronics case study you would probably put together a matrix similar to Figure 5 overleaf.

British Electronics analysis

	Our position	Their position
Strengths	1. This represents between £6m and £8m of business. 2. This gives Oblo a "foot in the door" with British Electronics. 3. We have a fallback option in Korea. 4. This is a chance for Oblo to get into new technology. 5. Their Sales Director will not want to tell their MD that he has lost this one. 6. This gives them a chance to earn foreign currency.	1. They are successful in their existing markets. 2. British Electronics made the approach to them – could this be seen as a weakness? 3. How much do they know about our need to do business in Sweden?
Weaknesses	1. We are under pressure from our MD to give them the business. 2. We need product in eight weeks. 3. Do we own the intellectual property in PC3?	1. They are uncompetitive on labour rates. 2. They will know that this is new technology, therefore they are a risk to us. 3. They have no track record with British Electronics. 4. Swedish taxes are high. 5. Can they "tool up" in time? 6. Our existing suppliers (of PC2) have demonstrated their worth in terms of quality and service.

Figure 5

Key Learning Point

It should be remembered, however, that even hard data could be controversial. Look, for example at Figure 6, which highlights different perceptions of a supplier's profitability. There is the analogy of two prisoners in a cell, one looks out and sees the bars, and the other looks out and sees the stars. People will have different views of the same situation or facts.

The impact of perception in negotiation

	One perception...	Another...
Profits are high	The company is doing well, look at how much profit it is making.	High profits mean large tax bills, high expectations from shareholders and the work force, perhaps the company is struggling and has to show high profits to keep the confidence of investors and customers?
Profits are low	The company is struggling.	This firm has realised that keeping profits down (which is easy to do with shrewd accounting policies) minimises expectations from a number of parties who have an interest in taking cash out of the business.

Figure 6

Later in this chapter we will look at the need to think through an issue from the other party's point of view. This is critical if you are to pre-empt the real issues or problems that will arise during a negotiation.

Task issues: tradables

Clearly it is important in preparation to identify and value the tradable issues and positions of each party. This is particularly important in competitive bargaining.

Quite simply, this involves looking at '*What do I want, and what can I trade to get it*'. It is important therefore to attempt to make an effort to identify what the other party is likely to want and what you think they may be able to trade. Each of these tradables may have different values to each party, and therefore it is important to assess the respective value of each tradable for each party.

Figure 7 gives an example of a salesman's tradable planning for a negotiation with a customer.

Key Learning Point

Planning tradables

Tradable issue	Value to me...	Value to opponent...
Price	*The buyer is almost certain to ask for a discount...*	
	1% discount reduces my profit by 10%.	The buyer appears to be price focused. I may be able to go to 1% if I get something in return.
Settlement	*My cash flow could be a lot better at the moment...*	
	I need the cash in quickly; settlement terms are cheaper than an overdraft.	1% in seven days may give him the discount he seeks and as a large corporation he can afford it, but can his system raise a cheque in seven days?
Contract length	*The buyer typically places 12 month contracts...*	
	A long term contract helps me to de-risk investment in capacity which we are making next year.	A long term contract will relieve the buyer of the need to go to competitive tender next year, but will it mean that he wants a price variation formulae?
Lead time	*I have high stocks and can start deliveries quickly...*	
	Getting the product in quickly gets the cash in quicker for me.	It could relieve him of the worry of not having the material available by giving him the comfort of some safety time.
Quantity	*He has two sources of supply at the moment...*	
	I can give him a 1% discount for each extra 10% on the quantity.	I need to check how he splits the business, 50/50,60/40. I will also need to monitor that he takes what he says he will take – or should I offer a rebate rather than a discount?
Retention of title clause	*New terms and conditions...*	
	Our new accountant is looking for some protection should any of our customers have financial difficulties.	I don't think he will accept this. (Are there any other options?)

Figure 7

The key issue in planning tradables is to look at each negotiable issue and to decide upon the value to each party in the negotiation. From here most negotiators will decide upon 'entry' and 'exit' points for each of their tradables. (This is what I will ask for, and this is what I will settle for.) This leads to the definition of a settlement range on each issue as shown in Figure 8 below.

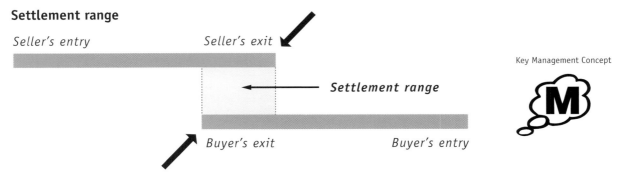

Key Management Concept

Figure 8

If there are problems in identifying a common settlement range, the easiest approach is to link two tradables together, for example, price and quantity, or extended credit for a sole supplier agreement.

Task issues: concession patterns

It is important that concession patterns are thought through in advance.

This helps to prevent the face to face negotiation including unplanned or larger than planned concessions, which may be more costly than at first thought. In a negotiation, if you are subject to considerable pressure, you may be tempted to offer a large concession. It is better to plan the concession pattern in advance and then stick to it regardless of the pressure you face.

Consider each of the following concession patterns and the impact they have on opponents. In each case the salesman has been told that he can give up to 15% discount, or 20% if he absolutely has to:

Activity

A.	No movement for a long time and then 15%			
B.	2%	5%	9%	14%
C.	3%	6%	9%	12%
D.	4%	7%	9%	9.5%

In each case what would you think the next concession is likely to be? The answers are given below. Thinking this through from the receiving end of the concession helps to suggest the right sort of concession pattern you should work with:

A. A large initial concession gives the impression that it is not a problem for the conceder and could create the impression that more is likely. Usually the first concession is seen as the start of the negotiation and not the end, therefore the buyer will keep pushing for more.

B. Increasing the value of the concessions as the negotiation progresses can have a similar effect.

C. Equally proportioned concessions will suggest to the opponent the size of the next concession, and will do nothing to stop the pressure from the buyer.

D. Reducing the value of concessions may create the impression that you are approaching your limit.

Key Management Concept

Planning concession patterns in advance helps to ensure that their impact is taken into consideration. The most successful negotiators make very small concessions, and don't give them but *trade* them. They will say for example, 'I will make this movement if you will do this in return.'

This way they are creating the impression that they have very little room to manoeuvre, and each move is linked to a concession from the other party. The fascinating thing about concessions is that most people do not value large concessions given easily in a negotiation as much as they value small concessions they have had to fight hard for. The trick in competitive negotiations is to concede very little, but get your opponent to believe that he has won a major victory in wringing that concession from you. This is a core skill in win/perceived win negotiations.

In a competitive team negotiation it is particularly important that each member of the team knows what the next concession should be, what needs to happen before that concession is made, and who is going to make that concession. It is amazing how often real negotiations produce situations where members of the team have different views on the size of the next concession that should be made.

In the British Electronics case study what would be the best concession pattern for the buyer, to move in pounds, tens of pence or pence? If the buyer had to move away from his goal of £5.80, what could he ask for in return?

Activity

Task issues: power

There is absolutely no doubt that power is a key topic in the preparation stage. Power is always likely to be the single most important factor in deciding the outcome of a negotiation. Thinking about your power and your opponents power is therefore a critical part of negotiation planning.

There are many different forms of power. It can come from a number of sources including custom and practice, financial resources, personal reputation or influence. Power can also come from expert knowledge.

There is also the ability to exert negative power, that is, the power to say no. In negotiations, it is often better to think about the power you do not want to have.

'Our company won't accept price increases for the rest of this financial year.' Another example would be; *'It is our company policy not to offer discounts.'*

In negotiation terms, power means either having an alternative, or the other party not having an alternative. Fisher and Ury (1) talk about power as your 'Best Alternative To a Negotiated Agreement (BATNA)'. Consider the British Electronics case study. If Oblo believe that British Electronics have an alternative source of supply, then British Electronics have the power. If the Managing Director of Oblo has told his Sales Director that agreement has been reached at MD level and the meeting is to tie up loose ends, then the power appears to rest with Oblo because the buyer now has no alternative. This also suggests that power may be perceived rather than real.

Key Learning Point

Power is never one sided and can be created through careful planning. In 1968 the Russians invaded Czechoslovakia and imprisoned the Czech cabinet in Moscow. On the surface, power rested totally with the Russians. President Svoboda of Czechoslovakia went to see the Russian premier and threatened to commit suicide. *'Whatever you say, the Western world will think that you have had me assassinated,'* he said. We will never know whether this was a bluff or not, but it is a tremendous example that shows that power is never totally one sided, and can be created.

Thought needs to be given not just to how to affect the opponent's formal position but also his personal position. Companies never negotiate; only people do this, and it is folly to ignore personal agendas. The buyer under pressure to meet a budget, the salesman under pressure to meet a target, both have personal agendas and pressures. The seller of a house who wants to make an offer on another property before it is sold, the buyer of a house who is under pressure from a spouse because this particular property is the one they want. All are examples which show that people negotiate and their personal situations and needs should be taken into account.

Task issues: the first five minutes

You cannot script a negotiation. You can never tell how the other party will react to your statements, your questions, and your demands. You can, however, script the first five minutes of a negotiation. These first five minutes are important for many reasons. During this period, you will effectively set the tone for the negotiation. You will begin to establish a rapport or working relationship with the other party.

Ideally, you will establish the sort of relationship where your opponent wants to work with you in resolving a problem. Unfortunately because of the first five minutes of many negotiations, a poor relationship is established where the opponent simply wants to solve his own problems and has no regard for you, and no wish to resolve your problems.

In the first five minutes, you will raise the issues in such a way that the other side will either begin to understand why they should work with you in solving them, or alternatively begin to consider the reasons why they should not.

How would you open the British Electronics case study in such a way that Oblo wanted to work with you to resolve your problems?

Activity

Process issues: making best use of time

These task issues are clearly important, but there is a body of research that suggests that there are some issues that stretch around the whole process of negotiation and which must be considered at the planning stage. The most significant research in this area was done by Neil Rackham (2) who looked at the differences between the behaviour of successful negotiators and average negotiators.

Rackham's research was based upon observation of 48 successful negotiators during 102 negotiations. The behaviour of these people was compared with that of a group of average negotiators. The definition of 'successful' was based upon the fact that:

- They were rated as effective by people on both sides of the negotiating table, including colleagues and 'opponents';
- They had track records of significant, demonstrable and quantifiable success;
- They were associated with low incidence of implementation failures. In other words, when they concluded a deal it was honoured by both parties.

Rackham split his observation into two, looking at the planning stage and the face to face stage. One of the most interesting facts to emerge was that successful negotiators do **not** spend more time planning for negotiations than average negotiators. What he found was a major difference in how they used their time. There were four major differences found between successful and average negotiators in planning:

1. Exploration of options

The average negotiator would identify 2.6 options for dealing with each issue in a negotiation, but the successful negotiator would identify 5.1 options, almost twice as many.

This suggests that the successful negotiator is more creative than his average counterpart. It is easy to understand how this relates to success. There is one major food producer, a household name, which when selling to the retail trade always sells at the same price. Does this mean that all buyers get the same deal? No, quite simply some are more creative than others.

One creative retail buyer takes the view that if he can't get a better price he will go for:

- A discount, *or*

- A rebate, *or*

- Twelve cases for the price of ten, *or*

- Extended credit, *or*

- A settlement discount, *or*

- The supplier paying 'rent' for the most attractive shelf space in the store, *or*

- More frequent deliveries (thus reducing stock levels), *or*

- Merchandising support (whereby the supplier displays the product to best advantage on the shelves), *or*

- Free mention of the retailer's name on TV advertising for the product, *or*

- A competition funded by the food manufacturer to customers buying the product through this particular retailer.

Thinking 'outside of the box' during the negotiation planning stage can often produce some spectacular results. Unfortunately in many negotiations we feel constrained by history, custom and practice, the way things have always been done in the past etc. One of the strangest pieces of advice ever given to a negotiator is 'When you do what you have always done, you will get what you have always got.' Loosely, this means if you are happy with the results you are getting, keep on doing whatever you are doing. If, however, you are looking to achieve better results, you have to work out what it is that you are going to do differently.

Key Learning Point

When looking at the British Electronics case study, there was a truly creative option that produced the most significant benefits.

2. Objectives

Whereas the average negotiator sets an objective for the negotiation, the successful negotiator tends to set three objectives. The successful negotiator will set an ideal objective, a realistic objective, and a fall-back position or walk away point.

If a salesman goes into a negotiation with the objective of achieving a 5 per cent price increase, and it becomes clear that this is not possible, where can he go? All he will be able to do is say that he failed. The successful negotiator will go into the same negotiation with a view of the ideal outcome that is possible. If during the negotiations it becomes clear that he cannot achieve this ideal, he will refocus on the realistic objective. If it becomes apparent that he cannot even achieve the realistic objective, he still has the fall-back position. If it becomes clear that he cannot achieve the fall-back position the negotiator knows that there is no point in continuing the negotiation.

The two most commonly made mistakes when setting objectives, are to set them too broad, or to set them in too much detail. Objectives such as to achieve the best terms, or to get the best discount, are far too vague and it is impossible to determine whether the negotiation has been successful when judged against these objectives. Objectives such as to achieve £30 per piece for 60,000 per month without giving any concessions on payment, or going beyond 10 per cent discount, or agreeing to sale or return, are far too detailed and constrain the negotiator by limiting the possible outcomes which may satisfy his genuine business objectives.

Negotiators also fall into the trap of setting objectives which have no direct link with their real needs. A good tip when setting objectives for negotiation is to set them in a form of 'I want … so that I can …' This ensures that the negotiator can understand the direct link between his negotiating objectives and their business objectives.

3. Common ground and long term perspective

Thirty eight per cent of comments made during negotiation planning sessions by successful negotiators refer to the common ground which exists with the other party. Only 11 per cent of comments made by average negotiators relate to common ground.

Key Management Concept

Eleven per cent of comments made by successful negotiators in planning sessions relate to the long term view of the relationship with the other party, whereas only four per cent of comments made by the average negotiator relates to long term issues.

There is a clear signal here that the successful negotiator places much more emphasis on common ground and long term perspectives than the average negotiator. It is as though the successful negotiator intends to emphasise the common ground and the long term possibilities, while playing down the differences of opinion. The average negotiator tends to play up the differences.

Does this make sense? It seems as though the successful negotiator is 'selling' the reasons why both parties should work to reach agreement. In playing down the problem, and building up the reasons why the relationship should continue, it makes it easier for the other side to understand the need to move from their opening position at the same time that the problem is being put into a different perspective.

4. Sequence planning

There is evidence to suggest that the many 'average' negotiators plan a negotiation in a rigid sequence such as price, then delivery, then payment terms, then contract terms etc. Problems may arise, however, if the other party is unable to discuss price and delivery without first of all talking about contract terms. The average negotiator has in this way backed himself into a corner unnecessarily.

The research by Rackham and others, suggests that the successful negotiator plans each issue independently. He is therefore able to deal with the items in any sequence should this be important to the other party.

There is also evidence to suggest that the successful negotiator, rather than going to a negotiation and putting an agenda on the table, will ask the other party what are the key issues that he would wish to resolve during the negotiation. In this way the negotiator understands the key issues facing his opponent and can therefore begin to think through how he can resolve both his opponent's key issues and his own.

Process issues: co-operative negotiations

In planning for a negotiation, there are significant differences between competitive and co-operative negotiations. The findings from the research on making best use of planning time would apply to both co-operative, and competitive negotiations.

Research carried out by Fisher and Ury (1) as part of the Harvard Negotiating Project team, suggests that there is another approach specific to co-operative negotiation planning which can yield benefits. Their approach involves looking at four key elements of a negotiation during the planning stage.

1. Interests

The Harvard team starts from the position that many of us take positions or postures in a negotiation, but these are different from our genuine interests.

The 'orange' example quoted in chapter one explains the difference between positions and genuine interests.

We frequently take positions in negotiation and these may not actually reflect our genuine interests. A buyer may fight for a discount as part of a negotiation when what he really wants is an advantage over his competitors. An assurance that his prices are better, and will continue to be better, than those paid by his competitors may be more appropriate for the buyer and the seller.

The Harvard approach is to focus the negotiation on genuine interests rather than on positions. You can test whether your objectives are based on interests or positions by asking yourself the question, 'Why do I want that?' This question usually leads to greater clarification of genuine interests.

As part of the preparation for a negotiation it is helpful to identify the key stakeholders to the negotiation and to identify their genuine interests. A stakeholder is anyone who has a genuine and legitimate interest in the outcome of the negotiation. The other party to the negotiation is clearly one of the key stakeholders to the negotiation and emphasis should be placed on trying to understand his genuine interests before the negotiation starts. This allows consideration during the planning stage of creative options which may satisfy the genuine interests of both sides. The other party may, of course, represent multiple stakeholders in his own organisation. The salesman may represent the accountant who wants prompt payment, the production manager who wants to clear stocks, the marketing department who want a reference customer.

2. Options

If interests are the problems we need to reconcile during the negotiation, options are the possible solutions.

One of the most common mistakes we make in negotiation is that we first of all try to figure out what solution we really want out of the negotiation, and then we see the negotiation as an exercise in selling that particular solution to the other party. This can lead to all sorts of problems. It may be, for example, that the solution we are trying to sell would not solve our opponent's problem. Alternatively, it may lead to the establishment of two positions, ours and theirs, and a compromise solution where we meet the other party half way.

If the compromise solution, is some arbitrary position along a continuum, it is difficult to decide whether this is a good solution that fully suits either or both parties.

The Harvard approach is used to look, not for 'how do I get greater movement from my opponents towards my position', but for how we come up with the creative solution which gives both sides greater satisfaction. This creative element of negotiation is often overlooked in the process of generating win/win options.

Key Management Concept

In planning for negotiation, the key is to decide upon not one, but a series of options which can be discussed during the negotiations. If you have managed to identify your opponent's genuine interests, then this should help to identify options which will satisfy both of you as part of a genuine win/win approach.

3. Alternatives: the *real* power

Not every negotiation concludes with an agreement, and it would be a mistake to believe all negotiations should end in a deal. It is often the case that you can do better by not reaching agreement and by walking away and pursuing an alternative solution. Alternatives are simply other ways of achieving something. This, in negotiation, means alternative ways of satisfying your genuine interests. In planning terms we are talking about identifying our best alternative to a negotiated agreement. The BATNA (Best Alternative to a Negotiated Agreement), and should help you to identify your walk-away point.

Key Learning Point

Once again, there is an element of creativity in thinking about how you may be able to satisfy your interests if the negotiation fails. The power of knowing what you will do if you cannot reach agreement is important. It helps to ensure that you do not close a deal on something which is not good enough.

Once you have identified a BATNA, it is helpful to spend time in the planning stage thinking about what you can do to strengthen this position. Improving upon the credibility of a BATNA is probably the simplest way of improving upon your own negotiating position.

Throughout this section of the book we have referred frequently to the need to consider the other party's genuine interests and positions. It is also helpful to consider their BATNA at this stage in the planning process. Forewarned is forearmed.

4. Legitimacy

It is common in negotiation to reach a deadlock or stalemate. Some commentators argue that this is a healthy sign which shows that both sides are fighting hard to achieve their goals. When a stalemate is reached some people try to resolve the difficulties on the basis of willpower. They take the view that being stubborn and digging in is effective.

There is a strong body of evidence to suggest that successful negotiators persuade their counterparts, rather than simply dig in. To persuade requires a degree of legitimacy for the point of view we are trying to get across. Preparing to persuade the other party means thinking in the planning stage about how we will show that agreement makes sense, and how your opponent can explain the agreement to the stakeholders he must deal with. This involves developing a legitimacy for your point of view.

There are three key forms of legitimacy:

Key Management Concept

1. The first is to use some external standards, both as a sword and a shield. As a sword, it can be used to portray your proposals as equitable and fair. As a shield, it can be used if your opponents proposals are not fair. If you can't agree on the value of a house, you can ask for an independent valuation; in a dispute you can suggest arbitration.

2. The second form of legitimacy is to use the fairness of the process to persuade. If you can demonstrate that the process you are following is equitable, does not discriminate between different parties, and will produce a fair and reasonable settlement for both parties, this will help move towards a successful conclusion to the negotiation. Following a declared process helps to remove any personality issues and bias from negotiations.

3. A final form of legitimacy is to offer the other side an attractive way to explain the decision to their stakeholders. This may involve taking some aspect of the deal and selling it aggressively so that the other party feel that they have reached a conclusion which they can sell within their own organisation. Often once a deal has been concluded you will often find one of the negotiators continues to sell the benefits of the deal to the other party. This helps to make the other party feel it is a good deal and helps him to rehearse the way he will explain the deal to his colleagues.

British Electronics: a solution to the case study

The real negotiation which surrounded the British Electronics problem outlined at the beginning of this chapter involved the application of many of the principles discussed in this chapter.

The relevant key points were as follows:

Genuine interests

British Electronics identified their genuine interests as:

> To win the Swedish Government contract, to secure supplies of PC 3 within eight weeks, and to continue their good relationship with the Korean supplier they had an excellent trading relationship with. Cost was also a genuine interest. It is interesting to note, however, that they did not see the negotiation as being about moving Oblo from one price to another.

Understanding the other side's genuine interests

British Electronics believed that Oblo's genuine business objectives were:

> To develop a trading relationship with British Electronics, to move into new technology areas, and to keep the Japanese company from building a manufacturing facility in Sweden which would inevitably increase competitive pressures. Profit was also taken to be a genuine interest.

British Electronics treated all of these Oblo objectives as assumptions, and the plan was to test the validity of these assumptions at an early stage of the negotiation.

Options

The buying team decided that they wished to pursue a co-operative form of negotiation. They did not believe that they would manage to secure sufficient movement on a Swedish price by haggling or applying pressure. They came up with three radical solutions which all had a co-operative strand running through them.

Common ground and long term perspectives

The plan was to emphasise in the first five minutes the tremendous opportunities which existed for long term business between the two companies.

The negotiations proper

The early stages of the negotiation were carried out in almost text book fashion. There was a degree of relationship building, a vision was put on the table which was intended to excite Oblo about the prospect of working with British Electronics, and a degree of information exchange took place. When British Electronics had reached the view that a working relationship based on trust was a strong possibility, they introduced the subject of the Swedish Government contract.

It was introduced in a very open way, with British Electronics saying that this was really the only reason they had made contact in the first place. Oblo, when asked if they had any influence they could bring to bear, agreed to use their political advisors, consultants and lobbying power to work in favour of British Electronics. This, if successful, may actually help to keep the Japanese company from building in Sweden.

Further bouts of openness and frank discussion led to the conclusion that the product could never be made in Sweden at Korean prices, but Oblo did agree to sub-contract production to the Korean supplier in return for a 5 per cent handling charge. This way British Electronics achieved a price near to the original £5.80, Oblo made a total of £300,000 commission and developed a good relationship with British Electronics. The intellectual property issues were removed. Oblo developed a close relationship with Kim Sun and later used them as a sub-contract source of supply for many of their mainstream products, at the same time acquiring an insight into the new technology.

Perhaps a better deal was possible, but all three parties concluded that this was a win/win negotiation that strengthened their relationships.

Summary and concluding remarks

Planning is often regarded as the unexciting part of a negotiation, but there is no doubt that the better prepared a negotiator is, the more likely he is to be successful.

As an absolute minimum, it is essential to consider:

- *Your genuine objectives;*

- *What you believe your opponent has as genuine objectives;*

- *The areas of common ground and the long term possibilities;*

- *The sources of power, or the alternatives which exist, and*

- *The tradables you have.*

To move into a co-operative negotiation requires additional consideration of your alternatives and the legitimacy you can bring to bear to your case in the negotiation.

Mastering competitive negotiations

Chapter 3

Compromise is usually arrived at during the course of bargaining. Although compromises may be worked out as a result of negotiating, the parties should not enter into discussions with the sole intention of compromising.

Nierenberg

All parties to a negotiation should come out satisfied. This does not mean give in; it means making the other man feel satisfied, even when he shouldn't be.

Machiavelli

This chapter explores the behaviours which are appropriate in the four stages of competitive negotiations. It provides a blue print which improves the probability of success.

Why can't all negotiation be win/win?

Chester Karass (3) opens his book *The Negotiating Game* with a tale of a bear who was hungry and a man who was cold. They decided to go into a cave to negotiate. At the end of the negotiation the man had a fur coat and the bear wasn't hungry any more. The story is used to illustrate the point that although we would like all negotiations to be win/win, life isn't always like that.

Many negotiations do not fit neatly into the win/win category. Far too many of the negotiations we have with clients, customers, contractors, suppliers and others are so complicated that we cannot always determine what is a fair result for both sides. In such negotiations, there is always the feeling that one side has won more than the other, but we can never be sure who has won the most.

We will discuss later in this book the steps that you can take to move many negotiations towards a win/win solution, but we have to be realistic; not all negotiations will be win/win. When a buyer comes in for a bigger discount, or a supplier comes in for a price increase, there is almost inevitably a win at someone else's expense.

Key Learning Point

This does not, however, have to be an antagonistic process. Most competitive negotiations are win/perceived win negotiations where both sides come away from the table feeling that they have won something. This is important if the two parties are to continue with a relationship. The essence of most competitive negotiations is to gain as much as possible, and to encourage the other party to feel that he has won. It may be, of course, that a straight trade is possible without any Machiavellian behaviour, but it would be folly to assume that all negotiations involve open behaviour and complete trust.

The phases of competitive negotiation

In competitive negotiations there are typically four phases. These phases usually overlap, and there will almost certainly be no explicit signals which say, 'this is now the end of this phase'. Nevertheless, it is important to understand which phase of the negotiation you are in. There are usually different behaviours that are appropriate to each phase, but many negotiators are unaware of the stage of the negotiation they have reached and use inappropriate behaviours. This can have significant adverse effects. A simple but frequently cited example may help to make the point:

Key Learning Point

In 1975 when the Americans and the North Vietnamese were negotiating an end to the Vietnam war, both sides met in Paris. There were different perceptions of how long the negotiations would take. The Vietnamese leased a villa for two years, the Americans took a suite of hotel rooms for a few weeks.

Six weeks into the negotiations, the Vietnamese believed they were still in the opening phase. They were still trying to establish the roles of each of the American negotiators, to understand which were the burning issues and which were the spurious issues. They were keen to test their assumptions and to understand the strength of the American position. The Americans on the other hand believed that they were at a much later stage in the negotiations.

Typically in negotiation, concessions come near the end rather than at the start. The Americans started to make concessions and the Vietnamese could not understand why. They thought that maybe the Americans were under time pressures and therefore in a hurry to settle, and so they slowed down the pace of the negotiations. Where you are in a negotiation matters, as does where your opponent thinks that he is.

The impact of time on negotiations

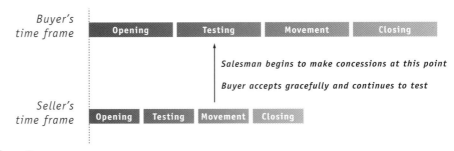

Figure 9

Action Checklist

The four negotiation phases are:

- The opening phase;
- The testing phase;
- The movement phase;
- The closing phase.

In each of these phases there are behaviours which are helpful, and behaviours to avoid.

The opening phase

The opening phase of the negotiation is the most critical. Although a negotiation can never be scripted, the first five minutes certainly can, and a detailed plan should be developed. The opening phase will set the tone for the negotiation. Both parties will set out their position and, to some extent, battle for the upper hand.

Key Learning Point

If the opening goes well for you, this will result in you having control, building the right sort of relationship with the other party, and will help you to test out your assumptions. If it goes badly, then you may find that you have lost control, have a relationship which is a liability to you during and after the negotiations, and you may give away any advantage you started off with.

There are four key elements of a good opening to a negotiation.

The right relationship

Relationships are rarely, if ever, neutral. In a negotiation your relationship will either be an asset or a liability. With a good relationship you can ask for something that you are not strictly entitled to, and you have a chance of getting it; with a bad relationship the chances are much less. If you wish to have a relationship that is an asset, you need to consider how this can be developed.

Action Checklist

The first phase of the negotiation should normally be used to put people at their ease and to build the sort of relationship that will increase the chances of agreement. Five minutes spent building the relationship will help to ensure that when contentious issues are raised, they are raised as part of a discussion that has some stability. Raising a contentious issue right at the start without developing the relationship will ensure that the other party is on the defensive throughout the negotiation.

There may occasionally be times when it is appropriate to open a negotiation by setting a hostile tone. The key is to make a conscious decision about the tone you want to set and then introduce the appropriate behaviours.

A sense of purpose

Have you ever been in a meeting that is badly chaired? Discussion wanders from topic to topic, there is no clear agreement on what has been said, sometimes people do not even know why they are there or what the meeting is about. Negotiations suffer from the same problems.

There is a need early in the negotiation to make the purpose of the meeting absolutely clear. If the negotiation is to stretch over several meetings, there is a need to make sure that the purpose of each meeting is explicit.

This helps to keep the negotiation focused and capable of being steered in the right direction. If it goes in the wrong direction, you have the means of bringing it back under control.

Common goals

Key Learning Point

Once of the common problems facing negotiators is when both parties have different goals from the negotiation. However much you are pushing towards your goals and objectives, there are always the symptoms of the other party working with you only as long as they can see their goals being achieved.

If the negotiation can be based on a shared sense of purpose, it is particularly powerful. If, in the first stages of the meeting you can define the outcome you are seeking in mutually desirable terms, this will help to focus everyone on common goals.

Consider a negotiation with a long-term supplier who has started in recent months to suffer from falling standards. There is much to be said for the buyer stating the purpose of the meeting as being 'to understand why the relationship isn't as good as it was, and to identify the steps needed to get it back to what it was.' A manager facing increasing industrial unrest could, in a similar way, open the negotiations with union representatives with the stated goal of 'trying to understand and resolve the underlying problems which are evident', rather than dealing with the symptoms of the problem.

Control and direction

In negotiations control is never shared equally. One side usually has greater control over what is happening than the other. Questions and agenda are particularly helpful in the opening phase as tools for gaining and keeping control.

Questions

Typically the opening phase in a competitive negotiation is one in which you are seeking to obtain more information from your opponent and are keen to delay the moment when you have to indicate your own position, or give information away. Probably the most frequently made mistake at this stage of the negotiation is to go in and set the scene. When you set the scene, you learn nothing, but the opponent learns a great deal about your position. Surely it must be preferable to invite the opponent to set the scene and explain how he sees things? This is often a problem throughout a negotiation, as people feel the need to take control by making statements or, worse still, speeches.

The man in control of a negotiation is not the man making the speech or giving information; it is the man who asked the question which led to the speech. Think about a barrister in court asking questions of a witness. Who is in control, the barrister or the witness? Clearly there is only one answer, and it is not the person making the speech.

Key Learning Point

A negotiation should not be like an interrogation, but if you wish to be in control, you need to recognise the power of asking the questions. It is also true that in a competitive negotiation, you may be giving your opponent control if you keep providing information.

Action Checklist

Key Learning Point

There are many different forms of question. Those, which at this stage of the negotiation are particularly helpful in getting further information, would include:

- The *open* question, such as 'How would you describe the situation we find ourselves in?' or 'What sort of customer base do you have?'

- The *probing* question, such as 'How would your proposal work in these circumstances?' or 'What is your available capacity?'

- The *direct* question which demands an answer, such as 'Will your company keep its delivery promises?' or 'Will you guarantee the quality?'

- The *leading* question, such as 'I can't think of another solution, can you?' or 'I have £800,000 of business to place, what are you prepared to do to get it?'

It is also helpful at this stage to seek to involve key members of the opponent's team at key points, for example, by:

- Turning on the silent, by saying 'You have been very quiet, I would appreciate your views on this.'

- Appealing to the expert, by saying 'You must have seen this problem elsewhere, how else have you solved it in the past?'

Open questions are the most effective way of starting a negotiation. At the earliest stage possible in the negotiation, you discover their perception of the issues to be discussed.

Questions can also be used at this stage to test out any assumptions that have been made. If you believe a supplier has high stocks or under-utilised manufacturing capacity for example, you could ask direct questions about stock or indirect questions about lead time.

In the opening phase of a negotiation, some discovery through questions is almost mandatory. It is important that you uncover the other side's complete shopping list, and questions need to be asked in this area. If you only understand part of their requirements, you run the risk of continually being asked for more concessions throughout the negotiation.

Delay indicating your position

It is equally important in the first phase of a competitive negotiation to play your cards close to your chest. A number of tactics exist which allow you to delay indicating your position. These include:

Action Checklist

- Testing understanding, for example, by giving back your interpretation of what has been asked, and then asking if that is correct; or asking the other party to clarify their question

- Appearing to misunderstand, perhaps by answering a slightly different question

- Answering a question with a question, such as 'Why do you ask?' or 'Is that important?'

- Ignoring the question, and carrying on without answering it.

Agenda

The agenda is a powerful tool for controlling a meeting or a negotiation. Once the agenda is set, there are rules for taking items in a particular sequence. Irrelevant issues or topics which are out of sequence can be put aside and a strong degree of focus is possible.

As part of the process of building a good relationship, it may be preferable to ask the other party what they want to discuss during the meeting. This is not giving control away, rather it is making the other party feel that they are part of the negotiation rather than 'having the negotiation done to them'. There is also a possibility that you will learn something about their priorities. Once they have tabled the issues that they wish to discuss, you can always add your own items to the agenda.

By the end of the opening phase you should have established the type of relationship you want, instilled a sense of purpose and taken control of the meeting, without giving too much information away.

The testing phase

The opening phase of the negotiation is often relatively short. The testing phase, on the other hand is usually the longest part of the negotiation. It is also the part of the negotiation that involves the most anxiety and pressure. It is during this often stressful phase that the benefits of having developed a good working relationship in the opening phase will be apparent. This phase of the negotiation involves a considerable amount of conditioning. Throughout this phase, you are trying to undermine the argument and the position of your opponent, and he will be trying to do the same to you.

Action Checklist

A wide variety of tactics exist to undermine the arguments of the other party. These include:

- Challenging any assumptions which they have made. If assumptions are left unchallenged, then this is tantamount to tacit acceptance that they are true.

- Querying facts. The testing phase of the negotiation has been likened to applying a brake to a moving vehicle. To leave assumptions and facts unchallenged is to allow the vehicle to keep moving. Challenging facts and assumptions applies the brakes to the other party's arguments.

- Pointing out omissions or inconsistencies. This is a further part of the attritional process which forms the testing phase.

- Warning of the implications or consequences. This is akin to putting roadblocks in the way of the other party. By pointing out implications and consequences of their proposals, you are making them less attractive, and therefore shaking your opponent's commitment to them.

It may be that in addition to challenging the facts and opinions of the other party, you need to challenge their credibility. This may sound contentious, but it is necessary in some extreme forms of competitive negotiation. Tactics to undermine the credibility of the other party would include:

- Questioning their authority. This could take the form of a Personnel Manager asking the Union representative if he has a mandate from his members for a particular form of action.

- Questioning his reasonableness. Most of us believe that we are reasonable people, and to be challenged on this fact, may result in a course of action being re-considered, particularly if linked to a challenge based on the implications or consequences of a particular course of action.

- Making a direct attack. There are a number of people who do not like the confrontational side of negotiation. Making a direct attack on them may cause a different course of action to be taken. It has to be said that this is a high-risk course of action.

- Quoting common practice. Custom and practice is a form of power based on the legitimacy of the way things have worked in the past. It is part of a suite of tactics which can be used to question the legitimacy of the other party's position.

Much of the testing phase of the negotiation involves conditioning. You are trying to condition your opponent that he is being unreasonable and is unlikely to succeed. He is trying to do the same to you. Whoever is best at conditioning the other person will get the greatest degree of movement when it comes to the next phase of the negotiation. Although this part of the negotiation involves the greatest risk of disagreement, it is essential that the challenges take place. Imagine a negotiation with a customer where a salesman puts an increased price

Key Learning Point

on the table. If the buyer does not react, the salesman may well come to the conclusion that the new price is not a problem for the buyer. It is important to note that even if this is not what the buyer is thinking, the seller may well have formed the view that price is not a problem, and this will make it harder for the buyer to get the price down later.

The message is, in competitive negotiation, you must challenge facts, positions, assumptions, consequences and even credibility, if you are to convince your opponent that he has to move from his current position.

In this phase of the negotiation there is a strong chance of deadlock if both sides work hard at conditioning the other party. This should not be a worry. Deadlock is the sign of a healthy competitive negotiation where both sides are fighting hard for what they want. Many people worry when they reach an impasse, and concede. This is clearly a mistake.

Deadlock produces stress, anxiety, frustration and even anger, but the negotiator should never lose sight of the fact that the opponent is probably feeling the same. Some weak negotiators will respond to deadlock by conceding. This encourages the other party to take a harder line. Never forget that the introduction of a deadlock may be a deliberate tactic by your opponent to test your resolve. The trick is to make the deadlock work for you. You can do this in many ways. One is quite simply by saying, 'So, we have reached a deadlock. What can you do to move us forward?' Even if this doesn't work, there is no need to worry. Deadlock has the greatest effect when it has been staring both parties in the face for some time. If you can bear the pressure for a while there is a chance your opponent can't and he may make a suggestion to move things forward.

If it is appropriate to break the deadlock, there are a number of tactics that exist. These include:

Action Checklist

- Re-stating the issue, then waiting in silence for a response. This keeps the pressure on the other party.

- Summarising the progress that has been made. This has the effect of emphasising the movement that has been made and effectively helps to play down the differences that remain.

- Focusing on signals such as non-absolute statements and responding to them. If someone says they don't *think* they can move or they don't have *much* more room for manoeuvre, you need to hear the possibility of further movement rather than the negative messages.

- Offering conditional concessions, but preferably with things that have little cost to you and great value to the other party.

- Pointing out the consequences for both parties of a failure to agree.

- Inventing new options for mutual gain. This creative approach is discussed in more detail in the next chapter.

- Changing the shape of the package under discussion (the time element, the specification, the payment terms, the quantity etc).

- In exceptional circumstances, changing the lead negotiator. This often allows a fresh perspective to be taken, or can remove any clash of personalities.

If the deadlock is still not broken, there are still a number of ways of moving forward. These are considered in the next phase of the negotiation, the movement phase.

The movement phase

This is the phase where the two parties move and come together. It requires the use of tactics to encourage or allow movement.

A frequently found problem is the inadequate negotiator who does not allow his opponent to move, or who criticises his opponent when he does move. Let me explain, if a buyer is looking for a 10% increase in benefits from a supplier it is unlikely to come all in one concession. What is likely to happen is that there will be a number of small concessions which, hopefully, will all add up to 10%. When the salesman makes his first concession, it is likely to be a small one; maybe 1%. A common response in situations like this is for the buyer to snort with derision, use words like 'peanuts' and say that it is unacceptable. If every time the salesman makes a small concession, the buyer reacts negatively, it is a behavioural slap in the face which will discourage rather than encourage the salesman to keep moving. A good negotiator will recognise that even if only a small step, that first step is a sign that the other party is moving. The trick is to encourage more movement rather than stop it. This can be done by:

1. Thanking the other party for the move;

2. And then saying that it is not enough.

This rewards the salesman behaviourally, but makes it clear that more is required.

Action Checklist

There are a wide range of tactics to allow or encourage movement. These include:

- Linking two items together, such as by offering to move on one thing if your opponent will move on another;

- Suggesting moving together, such as in some form of compromise;

- Hypothetically linking concessions, usually with words such as 'If I was able to do this for you, would you then be able to do that for me?'

- Using an adjournment to reconsider or to apply pressure to the other party;

- Re-entering the testing phase by applying pressure to weak spots.

Perhaps the biggest contrast between the testing phase and the movement phase is the speed at which things happen. Whereas the testing phase is often characterised by long silences, repetition and little apparent progress, the movement phase can be frenzied. Offers, counter offers, amendments, options and new ideas hit the negotiating table at a pace. It can be a mistake to sit in the negotiation and attempt to evaluate the offers on the spot. In most major negotiations, the consequences of misunderstanding the offer or not calculating the value of a concession can be significant. It is always worth taking a recess to consider a good offer at your leisure before responding. You do need to be careful, however, as this can create the impression that an offer under consideration is close to being acceptable.

The closing phase

The final phase of the negotiation involves making sure that the deal has been faithfully captured and accurately recorded. This phase is necessary to make sure that neither party feels at some later stage that they cannot live with the deal which has been struck.

Three actions are necessary at this stage:

Action Checklist

1. A comprehensive and accurate summary of the agreement has to be made. Nothing significant should be omitted.

2. If the negotiation makes the effort worthwhile, a written summary should be produced and sent to the other party for ratification. It is often beneficial if both sides can sign a written version of the summary so that there is no bias.

3. The agreement should be publicised to interested parties so that there is no misunderstanding of the content, or practicalities of the agreement.

These three actions will not guarantee that there are no misunderstandings, but they will drastically reduce the risk of this happening.

Summary and concluding remarks

Key Learning Point

Not all negotiations can or should be win/win. Many will inevitably be competitive, and frequently of a win/perceived win nature. Such negotiations involve four major phases which overlap. Each of these phases has a number of different activities and behaviours which are required if a successful conclusion is to be reached.

The opening phase involves developing an appropriate relationship, setting a clear purpose and beginning to control and direct the negotiation.

The testing phase is the longest and most tense and will involve argument and discussion. To be effective a negotiator must work hard at challenging and conditioning during this phase. Deadlock should not be seen as a problem; it is a sign of a healthy negotiation.

The movement phase is often short and involves the 'haggling' element of the negotiation. A trader mentality is important for this phase. Typically things happen very quickly in this phase, and it may be appropriate to slow the negotiation down by asking for a recess at any time when an offer has to be considered.

The closing phase involves summarising, recording and publicising the deal.

Where the negotiation is part of a long-term relationship, there is much to be said for sitting down at the end of the negotiation and de-briefing. The de-brief should be used as the initial planning steps for the next negotiation. You need to identify factors such as the limits of the negotiator's authority, his natural style of negotiation, the points you made which seemed to have impact and the points he made that you had not considered.

Mastering co-operative negotiations

Chapter 4

Two plus two is five

Ansoff

This chapter reviews the case for negotiating in a co-operative style and provides a methodology for win/win negotiations. It provides an insight into some of the actions that can be taken to move people from competitive to co-operative stances, and this is further developed in the following chapter.

Why co-operative?

The traditional view of negotiating is that both sides take positions and, after haggling for a while, gradually move towards their true positions. There are times when this leads to agreement and times when it doesn't. The process when described in these simple terms seems grossly inefficient. Why start from a position which is removed from our true goal? Why play what seems to be a game? Why risk ruining a relationship with exaggerated demands?

The development of co-operative approaches to negotiation recognises these weaknesses, and starts from a different point. This is based on the view that:

- The outcome should be a wise outcome, if agreement is at all possible. In many ways the term 'win' is inappropriate as it can encourage negotiators to see the process as a contest.

- The process of arriving at a solution should be efficient. The act of posturing and using tactics which conceal our true position can become a ritual which adds nothing to the outcome.

- The process should improve, or at least not damage the relationship between both parties. This is based on the premise that most negotiations are between long term partners who will negotiate again at some point in the future.

It is clear that competitive bargaining may not satisfy any of these criteria. One may win at the expense of the other; the 'game' may involve rituals and shams which add nothing to the process, and it is often counter productive in terms of the relationship.

The principal problems with competitive negotiating are that:

- **Negotiating over postures doesn't drive us towards wise agreements.** When negotiators argue over positions they tend to lock themselves in. These postures then take on a mystical quality. The more a negotiator discusses and clarifies his position, the more he becomes locked into that position. As more attention is paid to defending positions, less attention is devoted to meeting the underlying concerns of both parties, or finding creative solution to these issues. Saving face becomes a key issue as both sides feel the need to defend the positions that they took at the start of the negotiation.

Key Learning Point

- **Arguing over postures is inefficient.** It is not uncommon for negotiators to seek to improve their chances of securing an attractive deal by taking an extreme position, by using deadlock, by deceiving the other party or by stonewalling. Frequently, the more competitive the negotiation, the more extreme our postures and the more difficult it is to move away from them. All of these factors lead to inefficiency.

- **Arguing over postures puts relationships in danger.** Positional bargaining leads to a battle of wills which may be incompatible with the development of a mutually beneficial business relationship. The premise is that 'If I take an extreme posture and fight hard for what I want, then I will win the negotiation'. Unfortunately people take the process personally and goodwill is replaced by animosity.

Key Question

If being a hard positional negotiator is going to produce these difficulties, is the answer to be a 'soft' negotiator? The answer most definitely is *no*.

Hard, soft and principled negotiation

(based on the work of Fisher and Ury)

Hard negotiators are...	*Soft negotiators are...*	*Principled negotiators are...*
Adversaries who see the negotiation as a contest of wills	Friends who should not fall out with each other over differences	Problem solvers who separate the people issues from the problem being negotiated
Are tough and therefore demand concessions from the other party	Give concessions as a way of cultivating the relationship	Seek a wise outcome to the problem
Cannot discriminate between the people and the problem and are hard on the people and the problem	Cannot discriminate between the people and the problem and are soft on the people and the problem	Understand that the people issues need to be kept separate from the problem under discussion and consequently are soft on the people and hard on the problem
Proceed in a way which shows that they don't trust their opponents	Proceed in a way which shows that they believe in trusting their opponents	Believe that the negotiation should not be decided by factors such as the extent to which one individual trusts another, and therefore they proceed independently of trust
Dig in to what are often extreme positions, and fight hard to protect them	Take what they perceive to be a reasonable line and then concede relatively easily	Focus throughout the negotiation on interests not positions and invent creative solutions for mutual gain
Adopt tactics which include making threats, using bluff and brinkmanship	Believe that the negotiation is best helped forward by making offers	Takes considerable time and effort to explore both parties genuine interests and the extent to which they can be brought together
Believe that negotiation involves hiding their true position and may involve misleading the other party	Sees negotiation as an open relationship and consequently is open about their bottom line	Realises that if there is a creative solution, this may require not having a bottom line, but being prepared to consider any ideas
See the negotiation as getting the opponent to agree to their solution	Are happy to agree to the opponent's solution	Believe that the most sensible approach is for both parties to develop multiple options and choose later
Will insist upon their position throughout the negotiation	Will be more concerned with agreement than protecting their position	Do not believe in positions, but will insist upon objective criteria as a means of choosing the most appropriate solution
Believe that negotiation is a battle of wills and therefore plan based on the power they can create and apply pressure throughout the negotiation	Will yield to pressure, rather than run the risk of jeopardising the relationship	Principled negotiators are open to reason and yield to principle not pressure. They have no problem moving from their positions where this will lead to a wise outcome

Figure 10

Fisher and Ury (1) of the Harvard Negotiating Project devised an approach to win/win negotiation which is known as principled negotiation. Figure 10 opposite based on their work, shows the principal differences between hard, soft and principled negotiations. Look at the list and decide which you are closest to.

The principled approach is radically different in the sense that you are not planning on achieving a particular outcome or objective. Rather you are entering the negotiation, often without a specific objective other than to generate a mutually acceptable solution to a problem. This may sound unacceptable to many seasoned competitive negotiators, but it is no more than seeing negotiation as a genuine problem solving process. The key is to focus on genuine interests rather than postures or positions.

This is not the same as a compromise. Consider the orange negotiation between the two girls discussed earlier. Using the techniques of principled negotiation would involve a discussion on the genuine interests of both girls and would result in a better solution.

Fisher and Ury (1) propose a four stages process for principled negotiation.

1. Separate the people from the problem

People negotiate not organisations, and in any negotiation it is possible for people aspects to help or hinder. It is possible for egos, emotions and relationships to get in the way of the business issues being resolved. Principled negotiation involves accepting that both aspects of the negotiation, the relationship and the substance, need to be separated and treated differently. The relationship should not be allowed to become entangled with the problem.

The people 'process' needs to be dealt with as a separate part of the negotiation. This can be achieved by:

- Putting yourself in the opponent's shoes, and seeing the problem as they see it. This can you help you to understand the aspects of the problem that they are most anxious to resolve.

Activity

Key Learning Point

- Not making assumptions about their intentions and interests, but listening. Genuinely seeking to understand their point of view can do no harm in a negotiation, in fact it can do much for both parties, if it enables a solution to be developed which resolves all of the key interests.

- Not blaming them for your problems. Efforts must be directed at separating the people from the problem. Any judgmental views must be discarded; they will only serve to heighten tension and hinder the development of a solution.

- Discussing both side's perceptions. There will always be at least two different perceptions of one set of facts. Discussing them will move towards genuine understanding, avoiding them will perpetuate differences of opinion.

- Giving them a stake in the outcome by getting them to participate in the process. If you see negotiation as an exercise in getting the other party to accept your solution, you should expect to meet a degree of resistance. If, on the other hand, you encourage the other party to participate in the process you will experience a degree of buy-in to the mutually developed solution.

- Allowing them to save face. In fact it is usually productive to go further than this. Instead of simply allowing them to save face, there are additional benefits in terms of commitment to the deal if you can help them to rehearse how they will sell the benefits of the deal to the other stakeholders they represent.

2. Focusing on interests not positions

It is almost natural to discuss positions rather than interests, particularly when there is felt to be a conflict. This stems from the process of developing solutions prior to the negotiation and then seeking to impose those solutions.

Problem solving and principled negotiation demand that the problem is solved during the negotiation, and this can only be achieved by reconciling interests not positions. The six day war example quoted in Chapter 1 is an excellent illustration of this.

The Egyptian politicians wanted to save face with their people. They had lost the war and had no intention of going back home after losing the negotiations. The Israelis wanted security, some protection against a possible future attack. The creation of a de-militarised zone in the Sinai peninsula, which was returned to Egypt, is a superb example of what can be achieved when interests are considered rather than positions.

The key question for a negotiator to ask therefore is how do you identify and satisfy genuine interests? There are a number of tools that can be used for this:

- Put yourself in their shoes and try to understand why they are asking for something and why they would not want your solution.

- Accept that both sides have multiple interests. Although it is people not companies that negotiate, each person has to represent others from within his organisation. Organisations are complex and different individuals will have different requirements.

Key Question

- Acknowledge their interests as part of the process. Many arguments take place in negotiation simply because negotiators do not acknowledge the legitimate interests of the other party.

- Put the problem before the answer. Quite simply, this means do not go into a negotiation looking to 'sell' your particular solution to the problem. Before solutions can be proposed, it is important that all aspects of the problem are discussed and understood. Only then is there a chance that a proposed solution will have a good fit with the problem.

- Look forward not backward and so avoid blame and recriminations for past actions. It is difficult to keep the people and the problem separate if blame is being apportioned for past actions. By jointly focusing on the future, it is usually possible to be problem and solution focused rather than people focused and judgemental.

3. Invent options for mutual gain

The problem being negotiated is usually a common one. Even if this point is recognised, negotiators often fail to recognise that there may be many possible solutions to the problem. Similarly, they fail to recognise the need for multiple options. This flows from a fundamental human weakness where we believe we know the solution to any given problem. Unfortunately, inventing is frequently not seen as being part of the negotiating process. People see negotiation as being about closing the positional gap rather than broadening the options that exist.

There are many benefits to establishing a range of options and then measuring the degree of fit between each option and the needs of both parties. To secure these benefits it is necessary to adopt a different approach that requires:

- The separation of 'inventing' from 'deciding'. Rather than pass judgement on each solution, it is helpful to suspend judgement in the best problem-solving tradition. Passing judgement on each solution that is put forward at the inventing phase leads towards criticism and reluctance to propose solutions.

- Accept that the 'opponent' may have a contribution to the development of options. In fact, the opponent may have a better solution than yours. Encouraging the other side to propose is likely to be more productive than simply trying to sell your solution.

- Identify shared interests and dovetail differing interests. It is likely that in any deal there will be factors that are of different values to each party. The concept of trading by giving maximum value to the other party at minimum cost to yourself, will, if reciprocated, help to create value as part of the process.

4. Insist upon objective evaluation criteria

However highly you value an ongoing relationship there will almost always come a time when the harsh reality of conflicting interests emerges. No talk of co-operative negotiating strategies can conceal the fact, for example, that you may want a certain price and your customer wants it to be lower.

Deciding upon the basis of who has the strongest will can be costly, both in terms of the substance of the negotiation and also in terms of the relationship. It must be preferable to settle the negotiation on the basis of some objective criteria, which is independent of the will of either side. The solution must be to commit to reaching a solution based upon principle not pressure. Agreeing the principles on which a price can be set is infinitely preferable to a battle of wills. This opens up solutions such as market price, replacement cost, depreciated book value, manufactured cost or competitive quotation.

The more a negotiator brings equitable standards of fairness, efficiency or scientific merit to bear on a particular problem, the more he is likely to produce a package which is wise and fair, and which is free from a constant battle for dominance.

An alternative approach?

The *Getting to Yes* Harvard Negotiating model developed by Fisher and Ury (1) has received tremendous support as a methodology for conducting co-operative negotiations since it was developed in the 1970s and published in the 1980s.

Key Management Concept

Others have developed different approaches which have not had the same widespread acclaim. Bazerman and Neale (4) have developed an alternative approach which contain a number of principles which, although simplistic, do move negotiators towards a co-operative solution. The principles they propose are complementary to the Fisher and Ury approach.

They split their proposals into strategies for finding trade-offs and strategies for developing integrative agreements.

A strategy for finding trade-offs

If you start from the point of view that sharing all facts and information about a particular problem will lead to full knowledge and therefore rational decision making, it is not hard to understand the key elements of this strategy.

The strategy is based on building and developing trust and sharing information. Key to the process of gaining information is asking lots of questions. To develop trust may require information to be given away. Behaviours in negotiation, as in other forms of life, tend to provoke a mirrored response. Thus, giving information away in many circumstances is likely to lead to information being given back, and a more open relationship developing.

Bazerman and Neale also argue that instead of making an offer, negotiators should make multiple offers, and give the other party an opportunity to pick the offer which is closest to meeting their needs, or which is likely to yield the greatest benefit.

None of this contradicts Fisher and Ury, in fact there is a strong corollary between the two. To find the other party's genuine interests requires a questioning approach. Making multiple offers is also consistent with creative solutions for mutual gain.

Creating integrative agreements

Nor is the Bazerman and Neale approach to creating integrative agreements at odds with Fisher and Ury. The key planks in their approach are to add issues to the negotiation to the point where both gain a degree of satisfaction on some of the issues. This is further supported by the development of creative or radical solutions that focus on genuine interests. Once again, there is a corollary with the principled negotiation approach of understanding genuine interests and developing a number of possible solutions.

Co-operative negotiations with problem people

The approach to negotiation identified by Fisher and Ury has the over-riding advantage of seeming sensible, but there is an inevitable feeling that it cannot always work. It is reasonable to believe that there will always be people who believe in competitive negotiation and see no benefit in win/win. This may be illogical, but such people exist.

It is unlikely that any one prescription for negotiating will work every time. Co-operative approaches will certainly not work every time, but there are certain steps that can be taken to deal with difficult people before the approach is discarded. Ury (5) in a sequel to *Getting to Yes* has identified five steps that help to deal with difficult people who seem to have no interest in co-operative approaches to negotiation, and with difficult situations.

Key Management Concept

1. Don't react

We have all encountered difficult situations in negotiation. The opponent who gets emotive, becomes insulting or quite simply refuses to be logical. When faced with difficult situations like these we often either react, give in or break off the negotiation. Reactions of this nature are usually unplanned and the end result is a loss of objectivity.

The best approach is not to react, but to go back to focusing on genuine interests. To do this it helps to identify your BATNA. This represents the best solution you would have if you failed to reach agreement. In any negotiation this represents your power. Developing your best alternative in the planning stage of the negotiation, will help to keep your focus on the interests you are trying to satisfy and keep you away from what may be an over-reaction. Having a BATNA gives you the confidence and the detachment to rise above many difficult situations.

Other approaches can be used to help you with difficult situations. It may be helpful to:

- Buy time to think, perhaps with a recess, perhaps simply by not responding;
- 'Re-wind the tape' perhaps by summarising some of the key issues on which you have reached agreement, thus emphasising the positive rather than the negative;
- Refuse to make important decisions on the spot, thus avoiding the possibility of an over-reaction.

2. See the problem from their side

Putting yourself in their shoes is probably the last thing you feel like doing in a difficult negotiation, but it may be the only way to avoid moving into deadlock or a lose/lose situation. The key steps are:

- Listen actively by giving your opponent a hearing. This can have significant behavioural benefits. Evidence suggests that the more you interrupt and shout at people the more they interrupt and shout at you. Conversely, the more you listen to people, the more likely they are to listen to you, and understand you point of view.

- Demonstrate that you understand your opponent's position by acknowledging his point and the legitimacy of his feelings. This behavioural ploy can play a significant part in defusing tension.

- Where it will help to diffuse the situation, use open behaviour, such as offering an apology, or acknowledging your opponent's position and competence. This is not a sign of weakness. It will almost certainly help to defuse a situation and move the negotiation towards the point where rational discussion can continue.

- Summarise the points on which you agree. Once again, it is important to emphasise the positive aspects of the negotiation and the common ground.

- Avoid being provocative by building on proposals and suggestions made by the other party, rather than counter-proposing.

3. Re-frame the negotiation

Rather than rejecting what your opponent says, it may be helpful to re-frame it in such a way that you re-direct attention back to the problem you are trying to resolve. Imagine you have gone to ask a bureaucratic manager for permission to do something. What you want to do is clearly in breach of the rules and there is no doubt that if you ask for permission it will be refused. Can you re-frame the problem?

One way would be to tell the bureaucrat the end result you are trying to achieve and ask him how you could achieve it without breaking the rules. In this way you are making him part of the solution rather than part of the problem.

There are a number of tools that can be of assistance in re-framing a deal. These include:

- Asking problem solving questions which focus attention on the problem being tackled, such as 'How does your proposal get round this aspect of the problem?'

- Asking for your opponent's advice, and in so doing getting him to accept ownership of the solution to your needs, as in the example given above.

- Treating stonewalls, rejections and ultimatums as aspirations or simply ignoring them.

- Negotiating about the rules of the negotiation before returning to the substantive negotiation. This may take the form of stopping the negotiating and explaining that what is happening is not productive and asking if you can both come to some agreement on what the ideal outcome is to the negotiation.

4. Build a bridge

One of the most common problems in a negotiation is reluctance of the other party to consider your proposals. This may sound irrational, but there may well be good reasons for it. It is important to understand the possible obstacles which exist to the other party accepting your proposals. These can include:

- An ego problem associated with the fact that your opponent feels that it is not his idea, therefore it is not a good idea;

- Perhaps the proposal doesn't meet all the other party's interests;

- Your opponent may be suffering from fear of losing face. He may find it unacceptable to go back to his organisation with the deal which is on the table;

- Things have happened too quickly. Very often people are suspicious if negotiations go too quickly. There is a part of us which wants to slow things down just to make sure that there are no catches to what is being proposed.

Faced with a reluctance from the other party to accept our proposals, it is easy to push or cajole or pressurise him, and this may actually stiffen his resistance. In looking to move your opponent, the starting point needs to be *his* current position rather than the end position you would like to move him to. The key is:

- Involve the opponent as much as possible, particularly in discussion of the problem and then development of solutions. If he feels ownership of the proposal he will be more supportive of it;

- Ask for, and build upon, your opponent's ideas. Even silly ideas can be moulded and developed to the point where they satisfy both parties' requirements;

- At an early stage in the negotiation, ask for constructive criticism of your proposals and suggestions. If you understand the resistance early enough you can take the comments into account in re-shaping your proposals;

- Offer your opponent a choice of solution. Give him the chance to state which of a number of proposals is closest to meeting his needs.

Patience is often key at this stage. It may be appropriate to give your opponent an opportunity to break off from the negotiations to consider the proposals at his leisure. Frequently time to become familiar with ideas is all that is required.

5. Bring him to his senses, not his knees

If your opponent still refuses to come to agreement, there may again be the temptation to resort to pressure, and once this starts, it becomes harder to avoid moving to a battle of wills. Where power is used, and it should be as a last resort, the key is to use it to educate him rather than force him into submission. There are some techniques that can be used in these circumstances. These include:

- Asking 'reality testing' questions about the implications of a failure to agree;

- Discussing these implications without threatening, and re-framing the negotiation to deal with the problem of failure to agree;

- Demonstrating your best alternative to a negotiated agreement, but **not** as an overt example of force;

- Giving your opponent a choice;

- Never closing the door on the negotiations, but always giving your opponent that choice.

Even with the aid of these tactics, there will be negotiations which are not amenable to a win/win solution. The benefits which flow from co-operative negotiations mean that they must be tried before an alternative approach to the negotiation is used.

Summary and concluding remarks

Co-operative negotiations are intuitively and demonstrably preferable to competitive negotiations in the quality of the solutions they produce, the efficiency of the process they require and the development of the relationship they support. Although most people would agree with this, many have difficulty in putting a co-operative approach into practice.

Key Learning Point

The problem solving approach based on separating the people from the problem, focusing on genuine interests, creating options for mutual gain and insisting on objective evaluation criteria has proved to be successful in many different forms of negotiation.

There will always be situations where difficult people and situations lead to problems in trying to adopt a co-operative approach. Some movement can be gained by not re-acting and putting yourself in their shoes, by trying to re-frame the negotiation so that it focuses back onto the problem, by working with the other party rather than against him.

Where power is to be used it is always best to point out the consequences you are trying to avoid rather than to threaten someone. Above all, you should make sure that you go into the negotiation with an alternative solution should the negotiation fail. By finding and then developing this BATNA during the planning stage, you will effectively increase your negotiating power.

Mastering persuasion

Chapter 5

If you would work any man, you must either know his nature and fashions, and so lead him; or his ends and so persuade him; or his weaknesses and disadvantages and so awe him; or those that have interest in him and so govern him. In dealing with cunning persons we must ever consider their ends, to interpret their speeches, and it is good to say little to them, and that which they least look for.

Bacon

This chapter focuses on the approaches that can be taken to persuade people as part of negotiation. It explores and explains the six basic approaches that can be used, then goes on to identify a number of persuasion 'traps' and the steps that can be taken to avoid falling into them. Finally, it suggests some positive behavioural aids that can increase the effectiveness of persuasion techniques.

So why is persuasion important?

Key Learning Point

Whatever definition is accepted of negotiation, one element must be included, and that is the process of getting the 'opponent' to move towards our position. Whether we are looking at a competitive process or a co-operative process we need to move our opponent from his position to a position closer to ours. If we cannot get him to move towards us this will result either in impasse or in us having to move towards him. Persuasion is therefore at the heart of negotiation, and is a critical success factor.

Many people learn negotiation, and therefore persuasion, by experience. Through a process of trial and error we reach a stage where we adopt a persuasive style that works for us. Once a style or method is found which proves to be successful this is seized upon and used, usually to the point where it becomes a habit. The problem is that there is no one approach to persuasion which works every time. People are different, and therefore what works with one person may not work with another. Unless we have the flexibility to use different persuasive approaches we may fail to reach a satisfactory conclusion to a negotiation, simply because our style has no effect on our opponent. So what can we do? The simple answer is to develop a repertoire of persuasive techniques which will provide alternative approaches where they are needed.

How do we persuade people?

It is comparatively easy in a negotiation seminar to make participants feel uncomfortable simply by asking them to list the different methods they use to persuade people in negotiation.

Activity

Try it. Think of any negotiation you have to carry out, either a business negotiation or a situation at home where you are trying to persuade your husband, wife or children to adopt a particular course of action. List six different ways that you would persuade them to follow your wishes.

Persuasion techniques must be part and parcel of the negotiator's tool-kit if he is to be successful, and a negotiator without a full tool-kit will encounter problems. It is important, therefore, that we have the ability to draw upon a range of persuasive approaches.

Psychologists have classified the methods of persuasion that are available to us. They have identified six different types of persuasion. They are not new, and may appear obvious. Most of us will have used all six at some stage in our lives; but we usually use them without thinking about what we are doing. The key in a negotiation is that we must make a conscious choice as to which of the six we use. As individuals, we are susceptible to one type of persuasion above others, and the same holds true for the people we will be negotiating with. It is therefore important to match the techniques used by the opponent.

Let us now consider each of the six in turn.

Logical persuasion

Man is a rational animal, or so we like to believe. We have a society, legal system, business system and education system all based on logical, rational rules. This view is conditioned into us from an early stage in life and all through our education. Man has the capacity to reason and to be influenced by reason in ways in which the lower animals cannot; in fact, man is the only animal capable of rational thought.

There is no doubt that logic frequently features strongly in our attempts to persuade people. Some people use and react to logic more positively than others. Typically engineers, architects, accountants, scientists and others with a training in logical rules and principles, base their negotiations on logic. They will use logic and be persuaded by logic.

A logical approach to a price increase negotiation, for example, would be based around a breakdown of costs. A logical approach to a damages negotiation would centre on the actual costs incurred by the wronged party.

Key Learning Point

But there are far too many examples of man behaving irrationally for us to accept that logical argument will work on all people at all times. Even those who have a grounding in logical disciplines and backgrounds may act illogically. Man, for example, must be the only animal with a capacity for self-delusion, or the capacity to be taken in by advertising and propaganda. Often we believe what we want to believe.

Activity

Negotiations with monopoly suppliers or large bureaucratic organisations may see logic disappear quite early in the negotiation. Can you think of other business situations where the other party may refuse to accept your logic?

Logic does not have to be a meeting of minds and may not be a calm process leading to mutual understanding. Using logic in a negotiation may involve challenging facts and assumptions, querying data and conclusions. This may be quite tense.

To be an effective negotiator requires logical thought to be used as a means of persuasion, but also that we open our eyes to the fact that it may not always yield results. To believe otherwise will invite frustration. What is required is an understanding of the alternative approaches which can be taken should logic fail.

Power and co-ercion

When logical persuasion is having no effect in moving our opponent, this can often result in frustration which can lead to the application of power and co-ercion in an attempt to get our own way. Think about negotiations with children. Most parents start with a logical process which involves patience, understanding and explanations. If this fails the 'negotiation' can take a different direction, sometimes through frustration, leading to power and co-ercion.

Think about a negotiation you have had where you have started using logical, rational arguments only to find the individual you are dealing with somehow fails to understand. The frustration is often audible and visual as the tone of voice changes, and the body language shows tension and annoyance.

Power and co-ercion does not flow from frustration alone. There are also certain individuals and companies that opt for power and co-ercion as their style of negotiation without any attempt to use a logical process. Large multi-national companies have been known to adopt this style when purchasing. 'We are X plc, we are large, we are multi-national; if you want our business you will do this.' Individuals working within such a culture quickly pick up on this style, and it becomes self-perpetuating. Let us be clear; power usually works as a persuasive mechanism, particularly in the short term in achieving compliance. The two associated problems are that it doesn't always work, and in the long term there may well be repercussions.

Key Learning Point

It should be remembered that power is seldom one sided. Even the prisoner can hit back. It may be that a buyer using power and co-ercion will get his own way in the short term, but come a change from a buyer's market to a seller's market an abuse of power and co-ercion may well be remembered. The key question to ask in negotiation is, are you seeking compliance or commitment? Power is only rarely effective in bringing about commitment to a cause.

This is not to say that a negotiator should refrain from being positive or assertive. Negotiators at conferences and seminars talk about their toughest opponents and it is often pointed out that those who ignore the fact that the market is against them frequently succeed where others may even fail to negotiate. Persistence and assertiveness do seem to bring about a degree of success even in the most difficult circumstances.

Key Learning Point

It should always be remembered that power comes in many forms and can be created. A salesman at a recent conference spoke of the power of the NHS as a monopoly buyer of his company's products. He had been forced to accept low prices with minimal profit margins, and a degree of abuse from the ambitious buyer who dealt with him, for a number of years. Eventually he realised that a letter to his MP would cause questions to be asked at a time when the buyer was being considered for promotion. A fine example of creating power in a difficult position.

Where power does exist and is to be used in the negotiation, it is important that it is used to bring people to their senses rather than to their knees. Instead of threatening someone with a course of action, it is better to point out the consequences you are trying to avoid. Instead of a buyer saying; 'Unless you do this I will re-source the business', it would be better to say 'I am under pressure to resource the business, is there anything you can do to help me avoid this?'

The salesman dealing with the difficult NHS buyer was able to take this line in his discussions, so avoiding the need to write to his MP, and more importantly, without appearing to threaten the buyer.

Compromise

Compromise or splitting the difference is one method of gaining movement from your opponent but at the cost of movement from yourself on the same issue.

I once met a buyer who told me that he had read dozens of books on negotiation, and none of them were worth reading. He told me that if a salesman ever came in looking for a 10% price increase he simply argues with him for long enough and eventually the salesman agrees to only a 5% increase. He told me that this was obviously all that was needed in negotiation, because it worked every time. I would love to have to sell to that man. I believe that if I needed a 5% increase I know how I would get it.

Unfortunately many of us believe that negotiation is an exercise in compromise. We need to first of all differentiate between setting off with the intention of compromising, and having to compromise as the only way of reaching agreement.

In a negotiation there are always two opposing forces working on us. One set of forces involves us fighting to protect our interests. The second set is bringing us together because a deal is in both our interests. Figure 11 overleaf shows these forces. If in our particular case, the 'agreement' set of forces are stronger than the 'fighting' forces we are likely to be more concerned with reaching agreement than with protecting our interests. This will affect the quality of the deal we do. If in a negotiation, we believe that we will have to move towards the other party, there will be insufficient energy and effort directed at protecting our best interests.

Opposing forces in negotiation

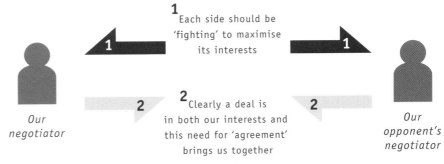

Figure 11

We need to make sure that we do not set out with the intention of compromising. Compromise favours the negotiator who takes an exaggerated position. The person who has taken an extreme posture in negotiation is more likely to benefit from compromise than the reasonable negotiator.

The effect of exaggerated posture on compromise

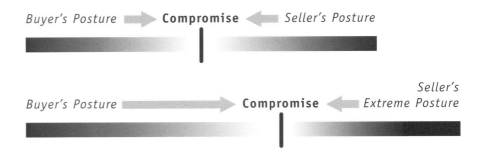

Figure 12

To some extent compromise may be viewed as abdication rather than negotiation. If both parties see the exercise as one in which they come to meet in the middle, then this is not a true negotiation, but a game in which a pre-determined solution is slowly reached.

A more positive view is that compromise is acceptable, but that it should only be used in the final stages of a negotiation if there is an impasse over a relatively small difference and no other apparent way of bridging the gap.

Mutually advantageous concessions

Trading concessions differs from compromise in that two separate issues are linked together rather than differences being split on one issue. It is usually better to exchange mutually advantageous concessions than to compromise. It allows both sides to make concessions that cost them little in return for gains which are of greater value. This suggests that concessions may be of different value to each party.

A simple domestic example may make the point. Anyone who has had to take an old gas cooker to a refuse tip will know the physical effort associated with this process. Getting a cooker salesman to take the old cooker away as part of the deal costs the salesman very little but is often of great benefit to the buyer.

Trading concessions is likely to be of great benefit if, for example, a sticking point is reached on price. At that point, the seller may be encouraged to move on price in exchange for a concession on volume, or terms of payment, or flexibility on delivery. Providing the negotiator has worked out a list of what he is prepared to concede and concedes these points in the correct order he may gain considerable concessions at very little expense.

It is in situations like this that the use of straw issues can be so effective. A straw issue is something that you ask for which you do not actually want. By asking for something early in the negotiation, you are able to trade it away later in

Key Learning Point

the negotiation in return for something which you do want. One insurance company told its top 20 suppliers that in future it was going to pay all invoices on a net monthly account basis, but that it would hold on to the VAT element and pay this quarterly. This is a perfectly legal thing to do and would allow the insurance company to earn interest on the VAT. Most suppliers were aghast at this idea. The idea of having to keep track and account for VAT separately and to make the necessary changes to their computer systems and procedures was frightening. Eventually after much hard negotiation, the insurance company agreed to carry on with their present arrangements in return for an extra 0.5% discount. The top 20 suppliers accounted for a spend in excess of £100 million and the use of this straw issue netted more than £500,000 for no change in payment terms.

Changing attitudes by the use of emotion

Many beliefs and attitudes are held which are not founded on fact and therefore cannot be shifted by logical argument. In the southern states of America, for example, it is still held by a small group of bigots that the Negro is inferior to the white man. Even in the UK there are still chauvinists who believe that women are intellectually inferior to men. These attitudes have no basis in fact but are unlikely to yield to logical argument, compromise, trading or even power.

Psychologists believe that with increasing age, our ideas and responses become more fixed and people build up a complex system of beliefs which form the basis of their actions. They, or rather we, will often defend them, more or less violently, against attack.

Similar illogical attitudes exist in the business environment and are defended as vigorously. We can all probably think of numerous examples at work or at home when trying to persuade someone of our point of view and we have had no success using reason.

If logic is not the mechanism to succeed there is one available to us in emotion. There is strong evidence to suggest that the arousal of any strong emotion may make the individual more amenable to suggestion. The negotiator who has the ability to invoke emotions such as anger, fear, hope, guilt, anxiety, pride etc. has a strong advantage. Salesmen are trained to exploit emotions in selling and the buyer who is unaware of this is wide open to this form of persuasion.

Anyone who has ever had a colleague cry in the office in a one to one situation will support the view that emotion has a powerful impact.

If you analyse the persuasive effect of television advertising, it is difficult to escape the conclusion that logic has no place in persuading people to buy TV advertised products. The advertisements tend to rely on different forms of emotion, or on humour which is intended to prolong the impact of the ad.

Key Learning Point

In a business situation, emotion is more frequently used than some may imagine. One computer company had an advertising slogan which said 'No-one has ever been fired for buying our computers'. It is not unusual to have salesmen asking for orders before a price increase comes through. At times of shortages most buying and stock piling is done out of fear rather than need. All of these are examples of emotion being used in business.

Emotion has a role to play in negotiation and we will build on this comment in later chapters.

Understanding the other side's genuine objectives and motives

Empathy is defined as the ability to understand why someone holds a particular point of view without necessarily agreeing with it. It is possible to bring someone round to your way of thinking by developing an understanding of what the other person is trying to do. As an example, Figure 13 overleaf suggests a number of alternative approaches to tackling buyer resistance to a quoted price.

Imagine that a customer has said 'Your price is too high'. The reasons for saying this are varied and the salesman needs to understand the reason before he can deal with it effectively.

Using empathy to persuade

The reason for saying the price is too high...	Possible approaches to overcome the problem...
I have better quotes	Is the buyer comparing like with like? Emphasise relative advantages of your offering.
It is higher than my budget	Find out the budget. Is there a contingency? Change the shape of the package (terms etc). If unavoidable beat the budget.
It is higher than I think the product is worth	Sell the benefits of the product
It was cheaper last year	Use logic, explain inflation etc.
I always say this to salesmen, it's my job	Pander to the buyer's amateurish behaviour without necessarily giving in
My boss said say it	Negotiate with the boss.

Figure 13

Key Learning Point

The most effective line that the salesman can take in the negotiation is to understand the reason for the resistance. In negotiation this works by understanding the problem which the other side is trying to resolve. It is important to remember, however, that we are talking about empathy not sympathy.

An important side effect of this approach is that it demonstrates a desire for understanding which is usually perceived as a positive behaviour by the other party. Instinctively, we know that the best way of striking up a relationship with someone is by talking in their terms about their problems, interests and ideas. We all warm to people who take an interest in us, and we are all capable of being motivated in this way. This is not advocating surrender or sympathy but that we demonstrate an interest in solving the other party's problems as well as our own. Empathy is the essence of win/win negotiations.

So what does this mean?

Anyone reading this book is likely to have experience of negotiation and of persuading people. We will have built up a style of persuasion that works for us, but unfortunately, it won't work every single time. There is no one style of persuasion that works every time.

If you are having difficulties in negotiation, it is worth stopping and making a deliberate choice of an alternative style of persuasion.

Activity

You should consider the natural style of people you regularly negotiate with and consider how each of the six styles would impact on the negotiation.

You should also consider your own natural style, and think about how this could be exploited by people you negotiate with regularly.

The skills of persuasion

As well as thinking about the styles or techniques of persuasion which exist, it is important to consider some of the skills which can increase the chance of each of these styles or techniques being effective.

These skills can be classified under the headings creating doubt and creating movement.

Creating doubt

There are three main techniques that can help you to create doubt in the mind of the other party.

1. Asking questions

Questions have an invaluable role in negotiation. They provide information, test understanding, give you time to think and can also be used to create doubt.

Questions that create doubt would include:

Activity

- Why do you need deliveries so quickly?
- Is this your only reason for not giving me an order?
- How do you reconcile that with what you said earlier...?
- How do you think we can increase the maintenance level at the same time that we reduce cost?
- Would you be interested in other approaches to solving this problem?

The intention of these questions is to gain more information on why something is so important to the other party, and to get them to reflect on some of the key issues in their arguments. It is important to recognise that it is more effective to create doubt by asking a question rather than making a statement.

Key Learning Point

The key issue with these questions is to challenge facts, opinions, assumptions, evidence, casual links and even, in extreme circumstances, the credibility of the negotiator.

2. Testing understanding

This is a behaviour that is intended to establish whether a previous statement or proposal was understood. In the context of persuasion it can be used to highlight inconsistencies, for example:

- Are you suggesting that as the new price then?
- Let me make sure that I understand what you are saying, you want additional discounts for a smaller system and without the other enhancements?

In addition to testing your understanding, these questions tend to challenge the arguments and statements made by the other party.

3. Quiet repetition

There is a strange power associated with calmly and consistently repeating the same message in a negotiation. It is the power of water on a stone. If a message is delivered again and again in a calm ordered manner it strikes home. Even a weak argument can be considerably enhanced by calmly re-stating an argument to the point where the other party has no doubt as to your views.

It is important in a negotiation that the other party is left in no doubt about some of the key messages that are given. It is always important to emphasise these key messages in summaries at the beginning and end of each meeting, but never under-estimate the power of consistently using the same phrase during a meeting.

Key Learning Point

Creating movement

At some point in the negotiation it will be appropriate to secure movement from the other party. This is usually when resistance is lower, either intrinsically

Action Checklist

or after creating doubt. There are three techniques that can be of help in doing this:

1 Questions about needs

It has been said that the best way to create movement is to show how a proposal of yours meets the stated needs of the other party. The first step must therefore be to seek an explicit statement of needs which can potentially lead to win/win outcomes. Examples would include:

- Am I right in saying that zero defects is a critical requirement?

- Are cash flow considerations your prime concern?

2 Proposing terms

Having identified an explicit need it should be logical to propose terms and state how these meet the need.

- We could defer 20% of the cost to next year <u>so that you</u> have sufficient left in your budget for installation.

- We can guarantee delivery within 48 hours <u>which means that</u> you will be able to reduce your stock levels.

The key words in these statements are the words at the end of each sentence which show how the proposal meets the needs of the other party. Expressing the solution in their terms explicitly helps them to understand the benefits of the solution.

3 Building

The research carried out by Neil Rackham (2) mentioned earlier, found that in 'low power' situations effective negotiators made great use of building techniques which extend or further develop proposals made by the other party:

- Good idea, we could then change the distribution channel.

- That could work, especially if we use bar coding.

The logic behind this is explained later in the chapter but is centred around the principle that agreement produces momentum, and disagreement stops the persuasive process. Research by Peter Honey (6) mirrored these findings.

Common persuasion traps

Very often we are responsible for stopping the 'opponent' from moving in negotiation. We make the basic mistakes associated with falling into a number of persuasion traps. There are probably five main traps to avoid when seeking to persuade an opponent to move. These include:

Key Learning Point

Making quick counter proposals

Think about a meeting where someone makes a proposal and immediately someone else makes a counter proposal. Who is the last person at that meeting to consider the counter proposal? Clearly the guy who made the counter proposal did not even consider the original proposal, so why should the guy who made the original proposal even consider the counter proposal? In extreme circumstances the proposer of the original idea may even look for reasons to criticise the counter proposal. People are at their least receptive to a proposal when they have just tabled a proposal of their own which has not been debated or considered.

If it is wrong to make a quick counter proposal, how should you respond to a proposal? The answer is to build on the original proposal, even if it is a long way from solving your problems. Successful negotiators will respond with comments such as 'That's an interesting idea, we could then build on it by doing such and such.' One way of looking at this is as if there are two negotiators trying to build a bridge over a river. If they both stand on their own bank trying

Key Management Concept

to build the bridge in a different way they will never succeed. If they start on the same bank and work together, progress should be made.

Wherever possible you should seek to build on the proposals made by the other party.

Loose words

Most of us have worked out that it is counter productive to insult someone in a negotiation. It inevitably gets a reaction. What many of us have failed to realise is that loose words in a negotiation can provoke a similar reaction.

Research by Rackham highlights the detrimental effect of gratuitously favourable comments like:

- This is a very fair deal
- I'm trying to be realistic.

Both comments are somewhat judgmental and the second is implying that while I am being reasonable, you are not. With phrases such as these, goodwill ebbs away slowly until a point is reached where co-operation is no longer a right or even a possibility. We have an obligation to ourselves to avoid judgmental words and phrases.

It is also true that other emotive words can take the focus away from the deal and into the realms of emotion. Imagine a negotiation where one party said something like:

- I resent being ripped off (when the opponent thinks he is being fair)
- That's not a sensible offer.

How easy would it be then to keep the negotiation on an even keel and prevent the wrong type of emotion creeping in?

The evidence suggests that such phrases provoke a reaction in a negotiation. It is not always an immediate reaction, and it may not be a drastic reaction, but some form of attack/defend spiral starts with each side gradually raising the temperature until either one party does something significant to bring the negotiation back on track, or goodwill disappears.

Inductive disagreement

There are times in a negotiation when the other party stops listening to what we have to say. The statement 'I disagree because…' may turn off the opponent as early as the second word. This is inductive disagreement. It is more than marginally better to use deductive disagreement ('When I consider …X and …Y, I can't see how this would work'). At least this shares your thinking with the other party before saying that you disagree.

It is much better still to disagree by asking questions. If you don't believe that something will work in particular circumstances, rather than say 'This won't work in these circumstances' you could ask 'So how would this work in these circumstances?' Your 'opponent' may help you to understand how it would work, or alternatively may come to the conclusion himself that it won't work. It is always much more powerful for the other person to reach a conclusion for himself than for you to tell him.

Low responders

One of the most difficult groups of people to deal with are low responders. These people tend not to give long answers to questions. In fact if they can avoid answering questions at all, they will. They also manage their body language in such a way that they do not give information away non-verbally.

There is considerable evidence to suggest that when we negotiate with low responders we feel uncomfortable with the long silences and lack of feedback and that we tend to over-compensate. We tend to fill the silences and do more talking. The evidence also suggests that we make more concessions and we make larger concessions.

Recognising the trap is three quarters of the battle. If you recognise that you are dealing with a low responder, you should make the effort to ask more open questions, to hold the silences which are caused by your questions, and to recognise the danger of making concessions. Sticking to the concession plan made before the negotiation, and insisting that concessions are traded are rules for dealing with low responders.

Timing

Have you ever had a brute of a day at work and a nightmare of a commute home in the cold and wet only to get in and one of your family starts asking for something even before you have taken your coat off? There are clearly times to ask for something and times to wait. Intuitively, we know that there are times to ask the boss for something and times not to, times to ask the family for something and times not to. Negotiation is the same.

There are two aspects to this issue. One relates to the timing of the negotiation and the other relates to the timing of key events in the negotiation.

Time produces different effects on the tenor of a negotiation. Businesses have times when they are looking to reduce stock levels or improve cash flow, departments have times of the year when workflow peaks, and individuals have Mondays, Fridays and the day before they go off on holiday. Before seven day and 24 hour opening, the supermarkets had times when they were prepared to discount fresh produce rather than keep it on the shelf over a weekend. All of these factors will influence a negotiation. Whether they should or not is another matter. It is important to think about the time you hold a negotiation; it does make a difference.

Within a negotiation, there are times when we should ask for a concession and times when it is inappropriate. The start of a negotiation is clearly the time to present your major requirements to the other party, as they will with you. It is clearly as important in a competitive negotiation, to get all of their shopping list at the start of the negotiation as it is to keep some of your shopping list up your sleeve.

Apart from this there are some general rules which can be applied in competitive negotiations. These would be:

Action Checklist

- Every time you have to make a concession ask for something in return;

- Every time a number is put on the table, stretch it in some shape or form;

- If the other party fails to meet your demands on a particular issue, always ask what else they can do to compensate;

- In a competitive negotiation, never be afraid of escalating your demands if they show weakness or if they escalate theirs;

- Never make a concession if you believe there is still a long time left for the negotiation;

- Never be afraid of 'nibbling' near the end of a negotiation. In other words when they think the deal is almost done, just ask for some little additional concession. Never buy a suit, for example without asking for a free shirt, never buy a video recorder without asking for free tapes.

Although, as with all general rules about negotiation, there are times when these tactics may not work, they will help to get a greater deal of movement than if the negotiation is conducted without them.

Persuasive behaviour

Peter Honey (6) has conducted a research programme that looked at how people react to certain key behaviours in negotiating situations. He considered, amongst other things, what we can do to shape other peoples' behaviour. His starting point was the assumption that there is a link between one person's behaviour in a negotiation and the response it gets. The links are probable rather than certain. For example if, in a negotiation, I hit you, you may either retaliate, break off negotiations, cry or adopt some other response. We cannot be certain of a particular response, but we can consider probabilities. By quantifying the responses he observed, Honey was able to calculate probabilities and begin to predict how people will behave in a negotiation.

Key Management Concept

Honey's conclusions are both scientifically and intuitively correct. At a simplistic level, for example, he found that when we seek information we get information 89% of the time. Low responders presumably accounting for the other 11%.

More significant findings from Honey suggest that when we make a proposal, almost 40% of the time the other party is likely to put obstacles in our way. These do not sound like good odds, and the question is what else could we do to improve the chances of reaching agreement?

Honey found that when we seek ideas, 60% of the time we get firm proposals and a further 20% of the time we get suggestions which are more tentative but can still form the basis of proposals. The message here is that if we seek proposals rather than make them we are more likely to get an idea which can move us forward. The skill then is in managing to build on this idea rather than reject it. When we then build on their proposals, almost nine times out of ten we get further information, support or further building on the proposal.

A framework for reaching agreement begins to emerge at this point. It works on the principle that asking for proposals and building and shaping them is more likely to lead to agreement than you proposing or counter proposing ideas.

The psychology behind this is not difficult to understand. Listening and taking the other party's views into account are more likely to build a productive relationship than some form of ping-pong game where both side put up ideas only for the other party to knock them down.

Summary and concluding remarks

The six techniques of persuasion have existed and been used in negotiation for a long time. Many of us will have used these techniques and I suspect that we have often used them without thinking. The important thing is to see them as a range of options. If a negotiation is not going well because you are failing to persuade your opponent, consider the options which exist. It is far healthier to say 'I am not using the right persuasive approach', than to say 'The other side wouldn't move any further'. Take responsibility for the outcome and consider how you could change the way the negotiation is going.

It is also important to recognise the persuasion traps which exist and make every effort to avoid them. Recognising the existence of such traps is three quarters of the way to solving them.

It is also important to recognise the way that people react to words and behaviours in negotiation. This helps you to understand the behaviours you should adopt if you are to move towards a satisfactory outcome.

Mastering power in negotiation

Chapter 6

I hold it to be proof of great prudence for men to abstain from threats and insulting words towards anyone, for neither diminishes the strength of the enemy, but one makes him more cautious, and the other increases his hatred of you and makes him more persevering in his efforts to injure you.

Machiavelli

Power can corrupt, but absolute power is absolutely delightful.

Anonymous

What power have you got? Where did you get it from? In whose interest do you exercise it? To whom are you accountable? How do we get rid of you?

Tony Benn

This chapter explores the effect of power in negotiation. It examines different sources of power and provides advice on dealing with opponents who hold the balance of power in a negotiation.

Does power work in negotiation?

There is no escaping the fact that power is the single most important factor in determining success in negotiation. There are no magic solutions for negotiating from a low power base against an opponent in a high power position. This is not a defeatist statement but a pragmatic statement of fact. Power works.

There are a number of things that a negotiator can do in a low power position, however, to improve the probability of success. The principles contained in this chapter are based on an understanding of the alternative sources and nature of power, research into how negotiators use power, and a series of practical approaches that can be used to defuse power in a negotiation.

So what is power?

Before we can explore how to deal with power, we need to understand what it is. First of all, there are a number of key points that help negotiators to put power into perspective.

Perception

Key Learning Point

The most important point to make about power is that it is illusory rather than real. If I believe that you have some power over me, then that is sufficient. If, however real your power is, I do not believe that you will use it, then your power is diminished.

In many cases perceived power and real power are totally different. In recent negotiations with a client, we were looking to reduce the supplier base for a particular commodity from five to three. Two of the original five suppliers were American and we decided that for strategic reasons we had to de-select one of these two suppliers. One of the non-American suppliers was in a very strong position, having monopoly manufacturing facilities in countries with high import duties.

Four of the five suppliers believed in the power that we had. The supplier who was able to hide behind the duty barriers believed it more than the others. Although we had relatively little actual negotiating power with this supplier, his perception was that we had significant power.

One of the two American suppliers steadfastly refused to believe that we would de-select him. His perception was that we did not have the will to use it. Consequently he refused to make the concessions necessary to stay within the supplier base and was de-selected. Our very real actual power had no effect in persuading him.

We need to explore the sources of power which exist.

The power of authority

Legitimate power comes from having a recognised position or authority. It may come from within an organisation, for example, being the Director of Purchasing. There is considerably more power associated with being the Director of Purchasing, than with being an Assistant Buyer. This type of power may also come from some other legitimating source. A contract gives both buyer and seller legally enshrined rights. Once the contract is in place it can provide a source of legitimate power for both parties in terms of what they can and cannot do.

The power to reward

Reward power is one of the two strongest types of power that exist. The ability to give or withhold something that the recipient wants or expects has a significant impact upon the way that people behave. Reward power is, however, based upon the desirability of the reward to the recipient.

Reward power needs to be understood in the context of both business and personal rewards. A salesman may receive a bonus from his employer based upon a targeted level of sales. The possibility of a buyer awarding a contract to his company may help him to achieve his target bonus, even if the contract to be awarded is only a small one. This gives the buyer the power to reward even if he only has a small amount of business to place.

The power of coercion

Coercion is the second of the two strong types of power which exist. Coercive power means being able to make threats about what will happen if your demands are not met. The comments made earlier in the chapter about perception of power are particularly relevant here. These threats must be believed, if they are to have any effect.

The power of reward and coercion, often go hand in hand. In the example given earlier, moving from five to three suppliers means that three suppliers will be rewarded with more business, and two suppliers will suffer by losing all of the business. Talking about three year rather than one year contracts can enhance the power.

Expert power

Expert power is often the most acceptable type of power. Based on experience or knowledge, it gives a speaker power over those with less experience or knowledge. When a salesman has more product or market knowledge than a buyer, for example, this can put him in a stronger negotiating position.

In a negotiation with a supplier, a buyer may feel at a disadvantage if the supplier's team includes a cost accountant who is able to explain overhead apportionment methods in a way which convinces the buyer that he has little choice but to accept the price.

Connection power

This is the power held by the Managing Director's Secretary. She has no legitimate power of her own, has little reward or coercive power, is not expected to have expert power, but does have access to the Managing Director. The power to influence by network or connection should not be under-estimated.

The power of information

In training programmes on negotiation, we often run a simple exercise in which participants have to buy and sell properties on a map in order to build a business empire. There is usually a point in the exercise where one central square is critical to each team meeting its objectives. All this information is available to every course participant because the map is on display on a flip chart at the front of the room.

Key Learning Point

There are occasions when the team owning this critical property has not kept up to date with the relevant changes in ownership of other plots. They are therefore unaware of the key role of this plot in the plans of the other teams. These participants will frequently sell this critical plot at a low price. On other occasions, those who have kept themselves up to date with changes in ownership will recognise the inherent value of this critical plot and sell it at a considerable profit. This is neither immoral, nor illegal; it merely reflects the power of information.

Charismatic power

There are some people who, simply because of personality or the sort of person they are, seem to be able to exert their influence just because of the charisma they possess. This charismatic power has been known to overcome other types of power in negotiation. Unfortunately there are no easy approaches to developing charisma.

The power to disrupt

This is the power to stop things happening, or to delay things. The power to disrupt is usually not apparent until it has been applied. Industrial disputes typically reveal the power to disrupt held by groups of society who are not considered to have any bargaining power.

The power to disrupt may be held by people who are quite junior in an organisation, people who have little authority but are required to implement decisions or to process transactions.

Some surprising findings

If power is the single most important factor in determining who will be successful in negotiation, there is some surprising news for those of us who may have to negotiate from a position of low power.

Chester Karrass (3) conducted a piece of research which suggested that *skilled* negotiators with power frequently do not use the power they have to full effect. In fact, the evidence suggests that skilled negotiators with power are often benevolent to their opponents. Skilled negotiators with power in a number of business situations were only slightly more successful than skilled negotiators with power. This suggests that while power is seized on by unskilful negotiators, it may not be exploited by successful negotiators.

Key Management Concept

The downside of this piece of research is that unskilled negotiators with power do tend to exploit the power, almost ruthlessly.

Karrass also found that power was particularly effective when negotiating against opponents who held themselves in low esteem. It had much less effect on negotiators who believed in themselves.

Hodgson (7) argues that this is a confidence issue. Negotiators with low esteem believe they will not get a good result, are therefore tentative in negotiations, come across as lacking in confidence or not having a good case, and therefore leave themselves open to exploitation. Her argument is that developing a positive approach to the negotiation, however much power you have, by developing your esteem will help to overcome any lack of power you have.

This at first may seem trite; so if you don't have any power just become confident! The question is how? Body language can be used to develop an air of confidence. When we are nervous we fidget, speak quickly, often in a slightly higher voice and appear too eager. Confidence can be feigned by locking yourself into a position, upright or seated, avoiding any unnecessary movement,

Key Learning Point

slowing down your speech and slightly deepening your voice, and making good strong eye contact.

There is also considerable evidence to suggest that when we plan for a negotiation we are more aware of the other party's strengths and our own weaknesses than we are of our strengths and their weaknesses. This can work in our favour if the other party does not appreciate their own strengths and our weaknesses. Figure 4 in Chapter 2 shows the type of approach which can be helpful in forcing our attention into the right areas when planning for a negotiation.

Key Management Concept

The work of Karrass and Hodgson therefore suggests that we should build a negotiating plan around our own strengths and the other side's weaknesses, and hold the negotiation anchored to these points. It would of course be folly to ignore our opponent's power, but it is equally folly to hold a negotiation on their terms when they have a powerful position.

Practical remedies for dealing with power

So far we have considered the alternative types of power which exist and some of the research which suggests that power is not always exploited in situations where we are dealing with skilful negotiators or we come across as being confident. But what if we are dealing with a negotiator who is determined to exploit his power to the full. What options exist?

There are a number of tactics that you can use.

Power can always be created

I was once involved in some negotiations on behalf of the National Health Service. One monopoly supplier had obtained a year's payment in advance and was refusing to make any sort of concession which reflected the fact that he had received tens of millions of pounds in advance of providing any services.

The negotiations were tense. The supplier consistently refused to give any ground whatsoever. Eventually we were able to create some power. At the time, hospitals were closing wards, operations were being cancelled, and urgent maintenance work on the infrastructure of some hospitals was being postponed. The press were very keen to print stories, and after the usual human interest and hardship angles had been fully exploited were looking for an unusual dimension to cover. The supplier was able to prevent a story saying that he was exploiting his monopoly position and was able to encourage a story which pointed out how he was funding a number of wards in local hospitals being kept open. Power can always be created.

Key Learning Point

The power of an alternative

Fisher and Ury (1) also believe that how we negotiate can make a significant difference to the outcome, regardless of the respective negotiating power of each party. They agree that there are limits, and that even the most skilful negotiators will find it extremely difficult to overcome opponents who have significant power.

Key Learning Point

The principled negotiation approach is to develop a good BATNA. Power is about having an alternative, or your opponent not having an alternative. If you are a supplier, and you are running at full capacity, then you have alternative uses for your capacity and have power. Equally if you are a monopoly supplier, your customer has no choice and once again you have power. The key therefore, to having power in negotiation is to develop your best alternative *prior* to the face to face stage of the negotiation.

When looking to buy a car, having an alternative means finding two or three cars you would be happy with. Then, in each negotiation you can have confidence in the fact that if this negotiation does not give you a good result, you have alternatives. Contrast this with a negotiation where the buyer has only found one car he likes and is effectively at the salesman's mercy in the negotiations.

The situation is just the same when negotiating a salary for a new job. If you have alternative offers of employment, you are in a much more powerful position. Alternatives do need to be actively developed in the planning stage. This requires a three-stage process:

Action Checklist

1. Creating a list of the actions you might possibly take if you fail to reach agreement;

2. Enhancing and developing some of the more promising ideas, and getting them to the point where they are realistic alternatives;

3. Selecting two, or maybe three, options that seem to be the most practical and the most credible.

It is always worth thinking about the credibility of these alternatives in the mind of the other party to the negotiation. As we have discussed earlier, power is perceived, and if the perceived credibility of the alternative is high in the mind of your opponent, it is more likely to be effective.

Just as important as thinking about your own BATNA, is to consider the alternatives open to the other side. To some extent, this means making assumptions about what they may be able to do. These assumptions should always be tested at an early stage in the negotiation.

Changing the package

An alternative approach is to change the package that is being negotiated. If you are negotiating with the supplier of a monopoly product, for example, change the negotiation to include a range of products that can be purchased from many sources. Consider adding other options to the package that is being discussed. If you have no choice but to negotiate with one particular product supplier, include maintenance or consumables or spares or repeat products which could be purchased from other suppliers.

Similarly, when dealing with a customer who is using power and coercion, consider changing the package. A supplier threatened with cheaper quotes from competitors may have no choice but to reduce his price. He may be able to seek to include other items in the package being negotiated so that he may recoup any losses he makes. This may include negotiating more realistic prices for subsequent sales, or reducing the credit period, or asking the customer to collect rather than have the product delivered.

The extent to which the package can be changed, depends upon the creativity which a negotiator can bring to the negotiation.

Key Learning Point

Change the time frame

In addition to changing the package being discussed, it is often helpful to change the time frame.

A few years ago, we were asked to assist a company buying a monopoly product in a situation where there was an excess of demand over supply. Our client was in a very weak position. It was beyond dispute that for six months there would be product shortages and no alternative supply available. It was also believed that in 18 months time a number of competing 'lookalike' products would start to come to the market, and the situation would change to one of oversupply.

The solution to this problem was quite obvious. We negotiated a three year contract with sufficient price flexibility when competitors came into the market. The supplier was keen to guarantee the distribution channel for his products over three years, and was prepared to discount supply for the first six months in order to achieve this.

Key Learning Point

Exploit the information base

If power is information, then there is much to be said for a detailed information gathering exercise as part of the planning process.

For a buyer, this may mean:

- Developing an in-house estimate of the suppliers costs, *and*
- Understanding his cashflow position, *and*
- Looking at projections of supply and demand over the foreseeable future, *and*
- Exploring emerging industries in developing countries, *and*
- Surfing the Internet to explore everything that has been published on a supplier, the product or the industry over the last 12 months.

For a supplier, this may mean:

- Understanding the buyers purchasing policies and procedures, *and*
- Ascertaining the authority levels of the negotiator, *and*
- Finding the genuine business issues facing others involved in the purchasing process, including those responsible for specification and those responsible for using the product.

Changing of the source of power

At the start of this chapter a number of sources and types of power were explained. If you are in a very weak position, simply because your opponent has a very strong power based on coercion, it would not be sensible to fight him on this basis.

Rather than take the opponent head on, it makes more sense to consider alternative sources of power. You may be able to consider, for example:

Whether you can appeal to the power of legitimacy. This may involve seeking to include the principles of equitableness or fair play into the negotiation. It may also be possible to invoke the power of custom and practice within an industry. A third alternative would be to invoke the power of the long term relationship between two organisations, which may now be under threat.

Whether you can use any expert power. This may involve putting together a strong, logical case based on statistical evidence, accounting rules and procedures, or legal arguments. In negotiating with an American company recently, we were told that they could not comply with our wishes simply because of a piece of legislation in the United States known as the Robinson Patman Act. The only way we were able to overcome this argument was to involve a legal expert in a negotiation who was able to explain and exploit the loopholes which existed.

Whether you have any other links into the organisation. This may involve exploiting business, social or personal links between the two organisations at a more senior level in the business. It is increasingly common for customers and suppliers in partnership relationships to have links in a number of business functions and at multiple levels within the organisation. Involving senior managers and directors within the business is not necessarily a sign of weakness, if it helps to achieve the business goals.

Ignore it

Power is often applied in negotiation through brinkmanship. This involves taking the other side to the edge and pointing out the consequences if he does not submit. It is a valid tactic in negotiation. However both parties need to recognise that it takes the negotiation to the point where the relationship may be irreparably damaged.

When threatened with power in the form of brinkmanship during a negotiation, the best response is to ignore it. To respond, will inevitably mean that the

Key Learning Point

negotiation escalates. If you are in a low power position, and your opponent is in the high power position, you are likely to lose. Ignoring whatever threats have been made and carrying on with the negotiation by re-focusing on business interests is the approach that is most likely to neutralise the tactic.

Develop an irrational option

Key Learning Point

It is sometimes possible to go one step beyond ignoring power and to treat it in a totally irrational way. A colleague of mine often tells a tale of a personal negotiation he was involved in.

His roof needed replacing, so he got three quotations. He opened negotiations with the cheapest contractor. The builder refused to do the work unless paid in advance. This seemed a totally irrational thing to do, the man was in a competitive situation, everyone knows it is never good business practice to pay a contractor in advance, and he seemed to have little or no power in the negotiation. Yet the man insisted that this was the only way he would take on the work.

He pointed out that he was once involved in a lawsuit to recover some money owed to him by a customer, and he now insisted that every customer paid in advance. He claimed that all of his customers were perfectly satisfied with the work he did and my colleague was therefore the one being unreasonable. The contractor invited my colleague to take out references, and they all reported satisfaction with his work. The man got his money in advance, did an excellent job, in spite of being totally irrational.

There are times when behaving irrationally, or simply refusing to accede to power, will produce results.

Put off the negotiation

There may be times when the most sensible option for a negotiator is to put off the negotiation until such time as the balance of power has changed.

A former Chief Executive of the National Coal Board once spoke about his tactics in delaying union negotiations from autumn to the following spring, thus allowing him to negotiate when demand for electricity was less. He had by then also taken advantage of the opportunity to increase his coal stocks.

Key Learning Point

One of our clients times his annual negotiations with suppliers, to coincide with the end of their financial year. At this time they are usually anxious to end one financial year with a contract which takes them into the new one on a positive note. He also allows them the opportunity to ship some of their existing stock into him, thus improving their balance sheet at the year-end. In return for this, he negotiates exceptional prices.

The balance of power changes over time, and will change throughout a business year. It is no more than shrewd business practice to identify the time of the year when a negotiation is most likely to yield good results.

Summary and concluding remarks

Key Learning Point

Power is central to the negotiating process and will have a significant impact upon the outcome of the negotiation. It is therefore critical that a negotiator identifies and develops his power prior to the negotiation taking place.

There are different forms of power, and at the planning stage a negotiator needs to identify any and all types of power which are available to him.

There are some approaches that may be of help when dealing with an opponent in a powerful position, but none can guarantee success.

Mastering commonly made mistakes in negotiation

Chapter 7

In a world in which some people gain or lose in interpersonal skills, some gain more than others. One factor which separates the winners from the losers is motivation.

Gurgen

This chapter describes some of the most commonly made mistakes in negotiation. It explains how they impact upon a negotiation, and provides guidance on how to avoid making them.

Why concentrate on mistakes?

Everyone makes mistakes. Unfortunately, when many of us make mistakes, the first thing we do is look for someone or something to blame. Psychologists call this attribution theory. We take the credit for things which go well, and find an excuse when things do not go well. There is a saying that we learn from our mistakes, but this can only be true if we take responsibility for the mistakes, and try not to make them again.

Many of the mistakes made in negotiation are relatively simple. They are common human failings which we all make at some time or other. Although these mistakes are simple, they can have a dramatic effect on the outcome of a negotiation. Research conducted by the author at the North West Regional Management Centre (8) identified 12 commonly made mistakes which seriously impaired negotiating performance. Continuing involvement in negotiations with clients has confirmed the widespread nature of these mistakes.

Removing these mistakes from a negotiator's performance will make a significant contribution to mastering negotiation.

A good negotiator stands back after each negotiation and asks 'What did I do right?', and more importantly, 'What did I do wrong?'. This chapter gives you an opportunity to look at your own negotiation behaviour and understand the mistakes you may be making, and more importantly, to begin to remove them from your negotiating behaviour. Introspectiveness is one of the skills of negotiation. If you wish to improve your own negotiating, 80% of the work is identifying the areas that need improving, and the other 20% is simply working on these areas.

These commonly made mistakes fall under three general headings: control skills, relationship skills and achievement skills.

Control skills

There are four basic errors surrounding control skills:

Questions

Have you ever been in a meeting where somebody said something you did not understand? There is a tremendous temptation in these circumstances to sit quietly as though you understood what was said. This is a common human failing. Very often we are afraid to show our ignorance, and rather than interrupt and ask a question we will sit quietly in the hope that we can catch up later in the meeting.

There is overwhelming evidence to suggest that in all business and social interaction, the most effective behaviour for taking control is to ask questions.

Questions serve a number of purposes:

- At a basic level, they provide information; (How does this work?)
- They provide opinions and perspectives; (What do you think the problems are they/we have to deal with at this negotiation?)
- They test our understanding of what has been said; (Are you saying that this product has unpredictable side effects?)
- They can put pressure on an opponent; (I have £800,000 of business to place, what are you prepared to do to get it?)

Key Learning Point

- Questions can also be used to give time to think; (Can you go through that again? I don't think I understand what you mean)

- Skilled negotiators will frequently answer a question with a question, and thus take control back; (Why do you ask?)

- But the most important reason for asking questions, is to take control of a negotiation. (Having dealt with price, what are your views on quality?)

In a negotiation, if one person is asking questions, and the other is answering, it is quite obvious who is directing the negotiation and who is merely responding and being lead in a particular direction.

The person who is controlling the negotiation is the one who is thinking:

- What areas do I want this meeting to cover?

- Do I have enough information on this topic?

- Do I want to change the subject?

- What weaknesses does he have which I want him to talk about?

He is then translating these points into questions for the opponent such as:

- Why are your labour costs so high?

- How is it made?

- Will you explain your tooling charge? I don't understand it.

- What stocks do you hold?

Research by Neil Rackham suggests that the most successful negotiators ask twice as many questions as average negotiators. In analysis of negotiations, he found that 20 per cent of all behaviours used by successful negotiators in negotiation were questions. When watching a negotiation, you can easily work out who is in control simply by counting the number of questions being asked by each side.

There are many types of question, all of which serve different purposes. Some questions, however, betray our dislike of asking them. Perhaps this is because we feel embarrassed, perhaps because we think the other party may be offended. The net effect is that we sometimes ask poor or inadequate questions such as:

- You couldn't reduce your price could you? (*answer* – that's right I couldn't)

- Is that your best offer? (*answer* – yes it is)

- You don't give discounts do you? (*answer* – no)

- Is there any way you could possibly see your way clear, to thinking again about your price, and maybe sharpening your pencil? (*answer* – definitely not).

Asking questions gives you information, time to think, and the opportunity to exploit the answers. First of all, however, we must learn to ask the right questions in the right way. You need to think about what you want to achieve, and then consider the best form of question and the most suitable wording.

Listening

We all believe we are good at listening, but how often have you witnessed any of these experiences:

Action Checklist

- A group of people in a social gathering. One is talking and another is leaning forward with one finger pointing and his mouth opening and closing like a goldfish. (Is he listening?)

- Two men both talking at the same time. (Can they both been listening?)

- Any group of people, each trying to 'out-do' the last story.

- An interviewer ploughing through a list of standard questions, not letting the interviewee answer any of them adequately.

Quite often when we think we are listening, what we are actually doing is waiting for someone else to stop talking so that we can have our say. Alternatively, we are busy thinking about what we are going to say next, rather than actively listening. What we often hear is what we expect to hear, or what we want to hear, as opposed to what is actually said.

Most people speak at a rate of 150 words per minute, and we think at a rate of 500 words per minute. This means that when listening to someone, our minds have 350 words per minute 'spare capacity'. How often have you found yourself listening to someone and your mind has started to wander on to other topics? This is a common problem. If it happens in a negotiation you will miss opportunities, signals, and insights into how the other party is thinking.

In negotiation, it is important to hear the qualifying words. Examples would include:

Key Learning Point

- Your price is *a little bit* high.
- I want *about* 5% off the price.
- I can't discuss cost breakdowns *at this point*.

In addition to listening to the words, especially the qualifying words, you need to listen carefully to the way things are said. There is a world of difference between the way something may be said if it has been calculated and considered in advance, or the way it may be said if it has been plucked out of the air. If a negotiator has not heard the difference he loses an opportunity.

The first step in improving your listening skills is to recognise that there is a difference between speaking, and not listening. A number of techniques exist for improving your listening skills. These include:

Action Checklist

1. Summarising and frequently 'testing your understanding' during the meeting. Periodically in a negotiation you should stop and test your understanding of what has been said. It is equally effective to summarise what you believe has been said.

2. Some people use the technique of instant repetition. This involves repeating to yourself what has been said, a split second after it has been said. This helps you to take in and retain the message.

3. Taking detailed notes is another useful approach which makes sure that you have captured what has been said.

Answers

Have you ever answered a question and then thought of a better answer? It is the sort of thing that usually happens in a job interview. When it happens in a negotiation, it can cause tremendous problems.

I was once told that there are two types of negotiators: those who can instantly come up with a superb answer after a question has been asked, and those who can't. If you fall into the latter category you need to think about your approach to answering questions.

Key Learning Point

When you have been asked a question, the first thing you should do is to consider whether you wish to answer it. If answering the question will put you in a difficult position, or will take the negotiation in a direction you do not want to go, then you should avoid answering the question. There are a number of tactics you can adopt if you don't want to answer a question. These include:

- Answering a question with a question. If someone asks you a question which you do not wish to answer, you simply say 'Why do you ask?', or 'Why is that important?', or 'That's a good question, what do you think?'.

- Making up your own question. This is a favourite trick of politicians, but it works just as well in negotiation. Asked a question about unemployment, a politician will give a wonderful answer about inflation, or the balance of payments, or anything except unemployment.

- American politicians are fond of 'putting something on the back burner'. This simply means 'I will come back to that later'. It is amazing how rarely the issue is resurrected in the interview.

- The power of silence. Frequently when a question is asked and there is a short silence, the interviewer will come in with a second question, or will clarify his question, or will begin to answer it himself.

This is a double-edged sword. You need to make sure that your opponent is not doing any of this to you during the negotiation.

Talk too much

Key Learning Point

There is a great tendency in negotiations, as in other spheres of personal behaviour, to make speeches or give our point of view or set the scene. Although some of this is necessary, what we are often doing is:

- Giving the other man information which may be of use to him;
- Giving him time to think;
- Taking the pressure off him.

It is amazing just how frequently in negotiation people start speaking and then don't know when to stop. The damage done to your case by even one careless word can be irreparable.

It is considerably more powerful if you make your point with a few well-chosen words, rather than launch into a long premeditated speech.

Relationship skills

Many books on negotiation tricks assume that you are negotiating with someone you will never have to meet again. This is one of the unfortunate consequences of sharp practice and skulduggery; you cannot keep playing tricks on people as part of a long term relationship. Most negotiations, however, are part of a long term relationship. A good negotiation, should improve the relationship between both parties, rather than jeopardise it.

Key Learning Point

There are four common mistakes made in negotiation in the area of relationship building.

Receptive to ideas

Frequently, we approach a negotiation having considered all the issues and developed a solution that satisfies our concerns. We then see the negotiation as about convincing our opponent of the value of our solution. The problem is that our opponent has also considered all the issues and developed a solution that suits him, and the chances of both parties finding the same solution are pretty remote.

Both therefore start the negotiation with their own solution which they wish to 'sell' to the other party. Each is resistant to the ideas of the other. Each solution may solve the problems of one party, but is unlikely to solve both sets of problems. As the negotiation proceeds, people tend to dig in to these positions, their solutions and their ideas.

It is relatively easy to break this spiral. The first step is to recognise that you are negotiating 'with' the other party, rather than against them. This involves being receptive to their ideas and their proposals, and indeed encouraging them. It is relatively easy to ask, at an appropriate point in a negotiation, how the other party recommends that you resolve the problem you are negotiating. The skill is then to develop, enhance and build on their proposal, to the point where it is an acceptable solution to both of you. Unfortunately what most of us do is propose our own solution, rather than invite theirs. If we don't like theirs, we then counter-propose.

Breaking the spiral starts from the basic premise that the other party will be more receptive to a solution based on *their* proposal than on yours. Even outrageous proposals from the other party can be modified, developed and enhanced.

Emotion

Emotion is a part of everyday life. There will be some people you will get on well with, and this will affect the way you negotiate with them. There will be other people you will not get on well with, and this will also affect the way you negotiate with them.

When you consider rows and arguments, it quickly becomes apparent that one side starts an argument and the other party is usually drawn into it. This applies to family arguments as well as business negotiations. There is a skill in only arguing when it suits your purpose. Having an argument in a negotiation is acceptable providing *you* choose to have the argument rather than you are the one who is drawn into the argument.

We need to broaden this out and think of emotion as more than rows and arguments. Enthusiasm, optimism, bonhomie and the willingness to work together are just some of the many forms of emotion.

If one person sets the emotional tone for negotiation, and the other is drawn into it, there is much to be said for being the person who sets the emotional tone, rather than being the one who is drawn in.

This means deciding in advance of a negotiation whether you wish the tone to be positive, motivational, enthusiastic or critical, negative and derogatory. You should ensure that having decided on the appropriate tone for negotiation you choose your words carefully so that you achieve the desired effect.

It is also important to consider how you should respond to the words and actions of the other party in the negotiation. It is all too easy to be drawn into an argument in a negotiation, when this was never part of your plan. The Americans have a saying, 'go to the balcony', and in a negotiation it may be necessary to go to the balcony when the other party introduces the wrong type of emotion.

Going to the balcony merely involves not reacting. When the other party says something provocative, you should mentally count to ten, and then continue by side-stepping what was said.

Words

There is no doubt that words are the tools that we use to build the right emotive tone for a negotiation. Words can inspire confidence, invoke a spirit of working together, emphasise benefits, and develop rapport. Alternatively, words can chastise, needle, alienate, and introduce personal animosity.

It is not the meaning of the word that is important, it is the impression it creates. Imagine a situation where a salesman is trying to sell oil to a motorist. He dips the tank. Then he has a choice, he can say the tank is half-full, or he can say the tank is half-empty. Which is most likely to sell oil?

I remember asking a strict Jesuit priest while on a religious retreat as a boy if it was OK to smoke while I prayed. The answer I got was very short and very sharp. A colleague of mine at a later stage in the day asked the priest if it was

OK to pray while he smoked. The different answer he got convinced me of the power of words.

Words can have a very positive and powerful effect. They can also have a very negative effect. Most of us will not need to be told that it is counter-productive to insult the other party as part of a negotiation. Although we do not insult the other party, we will quite often create offence by using a group of words which are known as irritators. These words are not intended to insult, but they do. They include:

Key Learning Point

- Poor and inappropriate humour, often attacking minority groups in society;

- Expressions and phrases which are not well received, however well-intentioned they are meant, for example, phrases such as 'dear' or 'love' used to address women or other phrases which may be received as patronising;

- Gratuitously favourable comments about us, our position, our intentions, such as 'I am making you a *very generous* offer' or 'I am trying to be reasonable' (and the implication is that the other party is not).

- Slang or swear words.

Although you cannot script a negotiation, you should carefully think through the impact of what you are about to say, and think about the best way of putting your point of view across.

Reading and using body language

Get into a lift, or on to an underground train, and watch where people look. We are told as children that it is rude to stare, and in adult life we frequently do not look at people enough in negotiation.

Key Learning Point

In presentation skills training we are told that up to 70% of the message that we give is through our body language. In negotiation we are constantly giving off signals through our body language, and so is our opponent. We need to make sure that we give signals that are likely to build and develop the relationship rather than those which threaten and intimidate.

Just as important, we need to make sure that we are reading the body language of the other party. If they are feeling frightened, worried, unsure, or defensive, we need to know so that we can decide whether to do something about it. If we say something in the negotiation that has a positive impact, we also need to recognise it. Unfortunately, many of us do not pick up the body language, and if even if we do, we do not interpret it anyway.

It is important to be receptive to the feelings of the other party in negotiation if the relationship is to be developed. One of the best ways of doing this is to be sensitive to the body language signals that are coming across, and to act upon them. Similarly, we need to make sure that we are giving off the right non-verbal signals.

The next chapter of this book goes into more detail on body language.

Achievement

Control and relationship building skills are a means to an end in a negotiation. The end is achievement. There are a number of 'achievement' mistakes that are frequently made in negotiation, and four in particular are worthy of comment:

Predictability

Many of us are creatures of habit. We have routines and rituals that make us feel comfortable. If, as part of a long term relationship, you have developed a particular way of negotiating with a trading partner, this will inevitably mean that he will be able to predict the way you will act and react. This will hinder your negotiating effectiveness.

A number of negotiators mistakenly believe that negotiation is an exercise in compromise. This encourages the opponent to start with an exaggerated posture so that he can achieve his objective and make the other party feel that he too has achieved a good result.

Others of us have favourite ploys or approaches to negotiation which may be effective if used occasionally, but lose their cutting edge when over used and abused. One public sector client when seeking to negotiate down the proposed price for consulting project always starts the negotiation the same way. 'My colleagues and I are really impressed by your proposal, however, there is another bid which is 10% cheaper. We would love be able to give you the job but need to know if you can match their offer.' Unfortunately for him, consultancy is a very incestuous business, and this man's reputation for this particular ploy has rendered it useless.

If you use the same ploys with negotiation partners again and again, you too will lose your effectiveness.

Argument dilution

In negotiation, when we build a case for our point of view, we frequently make the mistake of assembling a long list of arguments in support of our position. Unfortunately a case is only as strong as the weakest in a long list of arguments. If, in a negotiation, we put all these arguments on the table, a shrewd negotiator will pick on the weakest and use this to crack open our position.

Key Learning Point

The most effective approach to a negotiation is to have one very strong reason in support of a position, and to use only this argument in the negotiation. Other arguments may be developed in the planning stage, but should not be used in the face to face negotiation unless the strongest argument was found to be flawed.

There are times when it is better not to have any arguments in support of your position. A simple example may explain this point:

A retail buyer negotiating with a supplier quite simply said, 'Your price is too high'. This is a very powerful line to take in a negotiation, its power coming from its simplicity. The salesmen knew that he would have no choice but to discuss his price. Unfortunately the buyer then went on to say, '- At that price, I can't make my margin'. The salesman then proceeded to discuss all of the alternative courses of action open to the buyer which would allow him to make his margin, other than lowering the cost price.

There is a very old mnemonic, KISS. It stands for Keep It Simple, Stupid. It is a good line to take in negotiation. The simpler the argument the more powerful it is, the more complicated the argument the more opportunity your opponent has to find flaws.

Like to be liked

Although it is important to build a good relationship with your opponent, it must be remembered that this is a means to an end and *not* an end in itself.

The soft negotiator is more concerned with building relationships than achieving. In understanding this, it is also important to recognise that hard and soft negotiators are simply extreme ends of a scale, and that many of us fit somewhere between these two extremes. Many of us will therefore exhibit some of the characteristics attributed to soft negotiators.

Liking to be liked can have a serious impact on the outcome of the negotiation. There are four symptoms of this particular problem which are common in negotiation.

Aspirations levels

Research by Chester Karass (3) suggests that the most successful negotiators aim high. His research in the USA has been replicated in the UK. Two groups of buyers were chosen for a number of experiments. One group of young ambitious buyers were asked to negotiate a 15% discount off the range of prices from two suppliers. The second group of more experienced, but less ambitious buyers, where asked to negotiate a 5% discount off the same range of prices from the same suppliers. The outcome was clear:

- The experienced buyers all achieved the 5% discount. Not one exceeded the objective.

- Not one of the ambitious buyers achieved the 15% discount. However, all achieved more than 10%.

Unfortunately one of the many problems we face in a negotiation is the conditioning that comes with our experience. Because of our experience we may temper our aspirations. As we know a market or a product we tend towards norms and less radical aspirations. It is often the inexperienced negotiator who does not realise that something has never been done in a particular way before who achieves that additional benefit.

It is not just experience that causes the problem. If you compare the British culture with the Middle Eastern culture, there are strong differences in the way that we shop. These differences are carried over into our business lives, and the British culture is to see prices as fixed and non-negotiable. Many of us therefore do not ask for concessions which others may take for granted.

The message has to be aim realistic but high in negotiation.

Saying 'No'

'No' is a very hard word for some people to say. In price increase negotiations buyers often prefer to say, 'Why do you need the increase'. When asked for additional concessions, salesmen equally find it very hard to say no to discount requests.

We all need to recognise that the word 'No' is a legitimate word, and it may be the only word we should use at certain times in negotiation.

There will be times when it is better not to have the authority to negotiate, rather than to have the authority to negotiate. If your 'No' is non-negotiable, then you do not have to concede. If you have the authority to concede, you may well be pressured into doing so.

Soft words

Very often in negotiation we use words which take the edge off the message we are trying to give. A buyer will tell a salesman that his price is 'A little bit high'. Very often we will ask questions in a negative way such as by saying, 'I don't suppose you could give me a discount could you?'.

Psychologists say that if you use soft words words, the message is that you are not prepared to fight for what you are asking for. In a negotiation this is a clear and distinct weakness.

Silence

The power of silence in negotiation is significant. It is not uncommon to find that someone asks a question and then, when it is not answered for five seconds, the questioner begins to answer it himself. Alternatively, he may ask a second question, or carry on talking and ignore his own question.

This is a double-edged sword. In a negotiation, if you ask the question, you must make sure that any silence that follows your question does not prevent you from getting an answer. Similarly, if someone asks you a question, five seconds silence may be enough to ensure that you do not need to answer the question.

Impression management

In a negotiation you never know with any degree of certainty how far the other party can move. Similarly, the other party never knows exactly how far you can move. This suggests that negotiation is an exercise in impression management.

Both sides are trying to create an particular impression in the mind of the other party. In a business negotiation, the impression you're trying to create is, 'If I want this deal, I must move a long way towards his position in the mind of the other party to get it.' Unfortunately, there is another impression that is often created which is, 'This deal is mine, I don't need to do any more to get it.' What puts either impression into the mind of the other party? The answer is everything you say and everything you do in a negotiation.

Consider the following statements made by a buyer to the seller in a negotiation, and consider whether they create the right impression about the price or the wrong impression in a negotiation. Which way do they move the seller on the top scale in Figure 14.

1. Your price is a little bit high.

Key Learning Point

2. I have tried every supplier in the UK and no one has any stock available. You are my last chance. I know you have some stock. What price would you charge me?

3. You are the only people in this country who can meet my specification.

4. We have gone out to tender on your specification.

5. I have £800,000 of business to place, what are you prepared to do to get it?

6. I have met all of your competitors and if you come up with the right package at this meeting I will give you the order today.

7. I am under pressure to give the business to another supplier with a lower price, what can you do to help me give the business to you?

8. I do not understand why your prices are so out of line with all of the other quotations we have received.

Activity

Negotiation as an exercise in impression management

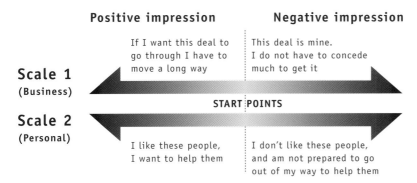

Figure 14

The first four statements moved the salesman in the wrong way on the top scale in Figure 14 while the second four statements move the salesman the right way.

The business impression that is created is only half of the story. People negotiate not organisations, and it is important that the right personal impression is created. In a negotiation it helps if the person on the other side of the negotiating table believes that he has a good relationship and wants to help you. Unfortunately, if the relationship is not a good one, and the person on the other side of the table does not want to help you, in fact, this will work against you. It is the individual on the other side of the negotiating table who will make a decision on whether to meet your demands. It does not help to antagonise.

This explains the second scale in Figure 14. To be successful, a negotiator needs to create the impression which moves the other party the correct way on both of these scales.

Summary and concluding remarks.

The 12 mistakes discussed in this chapter are basic. Nevertheless they are all observed frequently in negotiations, often negotiations involving millions of pounds worth of business.

Recognising that we make particular mistakes is 80% of the way to removing those mistakes from our negotiating behaviour. Consider the 12 negotiating errors, summarised in the lists below, and identify one from each of the three lists which you believe you most commonly make. Once you have done this, ask yourself what you are going to do to stop making them.

Control mistakes	Relationship mistakes	Achievement mistakes
Not asking enough questions or not asking good quality questions	Not being receptive to the ideas or proposals of the other party	Being too predictable
Not listening to what is said or the way it is said	Not being in control of the emotional tone of the negotiation	Diluting your arguments
Answering questions that don't help you	Not using the right words, and in fact using the wrong words	Liking to be liked, perhaps by not aiming high enough, not saying no, using soft words which soften the impact, breaking silences
Talking too much	Not reading or using appropriate body language	Creating the wrong impression on a business and a personal level

Activity

Mastering non-verbal behaviour

Chapter 8

As I get older, I pay less attention to what men say; I just watch what they do.

Andrew Carnegie

There's no art to find the mind's construction in the face.

Shakespeare – *Macbeth*

This chapter explores the way in which we give and receive signals with our body language. It provides an explanation of the eight major categories of body language and gives guidance on how to read non-verbal behaviour and how to give the right signals in a negotiation.

Is there a body of fact behind body language?

The subject is often considered to be a 'vogue' subject, but this belies the considerable body of academic research which has been carried out. The bibliography lists a number of specialist books on the subject which are built on a significant body of research.

It was Freud who pointed out that we often pick up a feeling about something in conversation with someone without understanding why. He believed that a subconscious message was passing from one person to another with neither party realising exactly what was happening. Freud was not the first to draw attention to body language; Darwin (9) explored the expression of emotion in man and animals. Others have gone on to build upon the early research which has been done, and there is now a surprisingly large body of scientific knowledge which supports the view that people's body language frequently gives away feelings, emotions and thoughts.

We are all able to read body language. When people lie, for example, they frequently give away signals without realising what they are doing. When we watch someone telling lies, we don't consciously register the non-verbal signals, but we register them sub-consciously. We get a feeling that something is not right. It is not just when people lie that we give off signals. Test this for your self; do you associate any particular non-verbal signals with:

Activity

- Telling lies

- Nervousness

- Lack of confidence

- Lack of interest in a speaker at a conference

- Impatience

- Particular interest, perhaps sexual, in an individual

- Extreme confidence

- Readiness to fight.

In negotiation these and other signals may be helpful to us, and we need to make a positive effort to pick them up. Although we are all able to read body language, many of us have not developed the skill. In negotiation there is much to be said for developing the ability to the point where we are able to make use of our body language and interpret that of our opponent.

Sub-conscious passing of body language signals from one person to another

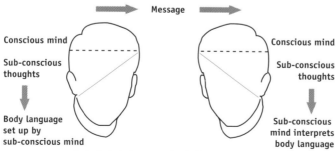

Typically body language signals do not pass through the conscious mind of either party.

Figure 15

A word of warning is appropriate. Non verbal behaviour cannot be read like a book. The gesture of arms folded, for example, is often quoted as a sign of defensiveness. It may also be an attempt to keep warm, or it may just be a comfortable position, or a habit. You cannot afford to look at one body language gesture and read it as though it must mean something.

Key Learning Point

The key is to look for clusters of gestures and particular behaviours that are well marked and signify 'loud' body language.

It is also true that people can learn to manipulate their body language to the point where it can be used to mislead. Actors do not simply learn lines in a film, they also learn to use a range of gestures and body language that are appropriate to the lines and the emotion they are trying to portray. It is possible for someone to act in a negotiation. All body language should therefore be treated as something akin to an assumption that must be tested.

There are some generalisations that can be made about the extent to which people give and receive non-verbal signals. Women are more sensitive to body language signals; it is believed that the ability to read body language is an integral part of 'women's intuition'. As we get older we tend to give off fewer signals. Similarly, as you progress through the class structure or a management structure, you find that people at the top of an organisation or in the upper classes, tend to give off fewer signals. We can all learn to be low responders and give away fewer signals. This can make it harder for your opponent to read you, but you should take care, it also hinders the development of a relationship.

To explore the extent to which you are already familiar with non-verbal signals, take the following examples and describe what you think they signify in non-verbal terms:

Non-verbal signal...

Someone avoiding eye contact while listening to you

Someone avoiding eye contact while speaking to you

Someone with a rigid unblinking stare, accompanied by a grim face

Someone rubbing his palms together

Someone showing their palms to you while they are speaking to you

Someone covering their mouth while listening to you

Someone covering their mouth while speaking to you

Someone stroking their chin while listening to you

Someone listening to you with folded arms

Someone standing at the front of a group of people with
hands on their hips

Someone blowing cigarette smoke upwards (as opposed to downwards)

Someone blowing smoke downwards

Someone moving forward quickly towards you across the negotiating table

Someone moving backwards away from you while at the negotiating table

Someone who 'mirrors' the behaviour of someone else within a group in conversation

Someone who refuses to shake hands with you when you offer your hand

Someone who orients their body away from you in a conversation

The answers to these questions will be found throughout this chapter.

The easiest way to interpret body language is usually to ask yourself how you are feeling when you adopt that particular posture. Projecting yourself into their body language in this way can help to develop a degree of empathy.

Activity

To illustrate the point that you can act using body language, it may also be beneficial to consider how you can give an impression non-verbally without committing yourself. How, for example, could you:

Establish an air of confrontation through the seating arrangement?

Defuse a potentially tense meeting by the seating arrangement?

Create the impression that a negotiation is coming to an end?

Make your opponents feel uncomfortable?

Once again, the answers to these questions can be found throughout the chapter.

Types of signal

There are three types of signal given off in body language:

1. Automatic responses which cannot be controlled. Blushing, crying, the pupils of the eyes dilating are all examples of automatic responses that cannot be controlled.

2. Overt and explicit gestures which are deliberately used instead of, or to supplement, verbal messages. Examples would include a hitchhiker with his thumb extended or an appreciative audience clapping.

3. Desmond Morris has described the third as 'body leakage'. This phrase denotes signals which are neither automatic nor deliberate, but which can be controlled if desired. It is this type of non-verbal behaviour that is most useful in negotiation. In particular we need to look for incongruence between verbal and this form of non-verbal language.

The eight categories of non-verbal behaviour

Non-verbal behaviour is said to make up almost 70% of all communications between people. There are, however, a number of sensitivity issues both for givers and receivers of messages which mean that this figure must be taken very much as an average.

Body language is not simply a human trait, animals give off and receive a number of non verbal messages; think of:

- A dog wagging its tail
- A cat hissing
- A puppy rolling on its back in front of an older dog.

All are part of body language and are used to send messages. In Freud's terms they pass from the sub-conscious of one party to the sub-conscious of the other without passing through the conscious minds of either. Many of us will sense non-verbal messages rather than read them.

In negotiation it is not enough to sense these messages, we must seek them out. This requires both an understanding of the messages and a positive attempt to see or hear them. In Freud's language we need to elevate the receiving from the subconscious to the conscious.

The eight categories of body language which are worthy of exploration include:

Facial expressions

This is the easiest form of body language to read, and it must be said, to hide. Smiles, frowns, blushing and crying are easy to spot and to understand. In a negotiation it is easy to make the opponent feel uncomfortable simply by frowning or adopting a low responder approach and avoiding any facial expressions.

It is worth noting that facial expressions are also important in developing relationships. Three points are worthy of mention:

Key Learning Point

1. To develop and build relationships, positive feedback is important. In a conversation this may take the form of nodding or perhaps a simple smile.

2. The view is supported in research by a number of authors identified low responders as the most difficult type of negotiator to deal with. When dealing with low responders people often exaggerate their concessions or say more as a way of compensating. Both of these actions are, of course, mistakes.

3. Michael Argyle (10) comments on a research programme carried out many years ago in which the facial muscles of a group of pregnant monkeys were cut, preventing the animals from smiling at their offspring. There was a marked and obvious difference in the relationships developed with their young between this group and a normal control group.

Gaze

There are two aspects of gaze which are worthy of mention:

Direction

People look at the things that interest them, and the direction of the gaze is therefore important. Pease (11) talks about three particular areas of gaze:

- The business gaze (which takes in an area between the eyes and the forehead);
- The social gaze (which takes in an area between the eyes and the mouth) and
- The intimate gaze (which takes in more of the torso).

It is interesting to note the effect on someone of the opposite sex of the wrong type of gaze. In a negotiation this can have a devastating effect.

Degree

The intensity of the gaze is also significant and three levels can be noted:

0 to 33%	Lack of interest in the speaker or the message when listening, and a lack of interest in the listener when speaking. It may also indicate shiftiness on the part of the speaker.
33% to 66%	This is the norm for both listening and speaking. Both speaker and listener feel comfortable in this zone.
66% to 100%	Intensity of gaze may indicate particular interest or hostility.

The easiest way to build a relationship with someone at the start of a negotiation is to smile at him or her and make good eye contact.

Key Learning Point

Gestures

This is the most fruitful area of body language. Eight categories of gestures are obvious:

Palm gestures

Open palm gestures typically demonstrate honesty, and this has come to be ritualised in court proceedings, where witnesses are asked to raise their hand and show their palms when swearing to tell the truth.

Closed or hidden palm gestures are often indicative of secrecy or a desire to hide something, and are frequently found with children. They are therefore, some of the many gestures which may indicate that a lie is being told.

Sales training programmes often focus on the need to look for buying signals. Salesmen are trained to watch for the exposed palms as a buying signal. Thus if a buyer is giving a salesman half a dozen reasons why he won't get the order, the salesman will watch for the one reason which is accompanied by the palms being revealed.

Hand and arm gestures

Rubbing palms is a typical sign of a positive expectation, be it a waiter expecting a tip, a salesman expecting an order or a buyer expecting a gift at Christmas.

Hand clenching is a typical sign of frustration, and the height at which the hands are held is an indication of the strength of the frustration; the higher the hands the more difficult it is to deal with.

Steepling is a sign of confidence, frequently found in superior/subordinate discussions. Men tend to steeple much more overtly than women.

Steepling

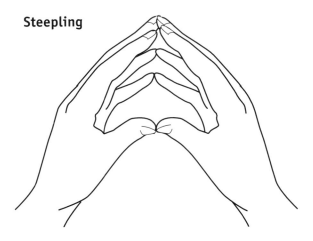

Figure 16

Gripping hands, arms and wrists

Gripping hands is typically a confidence gesture; gripping hands behind the back, with chest out is taught at presentation skills courses as a gesture which shows confidence. Making a presentation with hands behind the back tends to display a confident authoritative style. Some women, however, find this to be both physically and psychologically uncomfortable.

Gripping the wrists is a slightly different gesture, and one which is held to be a sign of frustration which is being kept in control.

Thumb displays

In palmistry the thumb is an indicator of dominance. In body language it also typifies dominance or a feeling of superiority. A thumb display may be found, for example, in barristers gripping their gowns at chest height, or in arrogant individuals where they show their thumbs over the waist bands of their trousers.

Hand to face gestures

Generally hand to face gestures indicate doubt, deceit or uncertainty; although there are some exceptions to this which need to be borne in mind.

The hand across the mouth for example, typifies someone speaking who is either not confident with what he is saying or is uncomfortable with what he is saying – possibly because it is bad news or possibly because it is not true.

Similarly while listening, the hand across the mouth indicates doubt or disbelief.

The hand to the nose is a less obvious form of hand to mouth gesture. Desmond Morris talks about the nose or scalp scratch as indicators of someone telling lies. This is based on the fact that when we lie we are nervous and the body generates small electrical charges that pass all over the body. The three most sensitive parts of the body are the nose, the ear and the scalp, which is why when we lie we often scratch our nose, or scratch our forehead. The point must be emphasised again that you cannot read one gesture and reach a conclusion. All signals received should be treated as assumptions.

The neck scratch represents uncertainty or discomfort with what is being said. The message from a listener is 'convince me', from a speaker it is a lack of confidence.

Fingers, or objects such as pencils, in the mouth show a need for re-assurance, particularly under pressure.

Pointing, either with fingers or pencils and other objects, is a sign of aggression. If an opponent in a negotiation has been quiet for ten or twenty minutes and then suddenly starts pointing a pencil across the table, then something has upset him. Frequently something like this will be accompanied with a move across the table. Recognising the signal gives you an opportunity to defuse the tension.

Hand to cheek gestures may be one of two things:

- If the hand is supporting the head it is boredom;
- If it is not supportive, and the head is held at an angle, and a finger is pointing upwards, it may be an evaluative gesture.

Chin stroking, or cleaning glasses is also an evaluation gesture, often just before a decision is to be taken.

Arm barriers

Typically arm barriers are defensive and/or are intended to block out unwelcome messages. Where the folded arms are re-inforced by hands gripping the arms this is a hostile gesture. Some organisations will teach their sales force to respond to this by getting customers to open their arms, possibly by offering a piece of paper or a brochure. It is as though breaking the body language will open the mind of the customer.

There are a number of disguised arm crosses that include:

- Touching the cuffs of the sleeves;
- Carrying a clipboard, a file, a bunch of flowers or a handbag in front of the body.

Crossing the legs is another form of arm barrier, as is fastening the button on a jacket. A lecturer or presenter standing behind a desk or a rostrum is also indicating the need for a barrier between him and the audience.

Other gestures

The gesture is the most common form of body language and there are so many of them. The gestures covered so far are the most commonly found but others cannot be ignored. There is, for example:

The gesture... which indicates...

Straddling a chair:	...a feeling of dominance
Head gestures:	...amongst which yes and no are the most obvious
	...head held high which indicates confidence
	...head down which indicates disapproval
	...head held at an angle which indicates interest
	...hands behind the head which indicates a feeling of control
Hands on hips:	...which at the start of a presentation, for example, indicates a high achiever or someone who intends to take control
The praying mantis (coming to the edge of a seat)	...which indicates expectation position
Tapping or drumming the fingers	...which indicates impatience
Blowing cigarette smoke upwards	...which indicates confidence and open-ness
Blowing cigarette smoke down	...which indicates a tendency towards secretiveness.

Posture

There are four issues to discuss in relation to posture:

Typically leaning forward indicates attentiveness. The man at a meeting who is leaning forward is likely to be the man who is keen to move things forward and get a decision.

Typically leaning back indicates a desire to withdraw from the proceedings, or to take the time to consider what has just been said. In a negotiation, if someone sits back after you have just said something it may be worthwhile asking them how they feel about what you have said.

Normally you would expect someone walking with a 'collapsed' posture to indicate depression, lack of confidence or dissatisfaction with life or something in particular. A 'puffed up' posture, such as a military walk or swagger on the other hand, would indicate confidence.

'Mirror imaging' is a particular behaviour worthy of mention. This is where one person adopts the posture of someone else he is in conversation with. It portrays a sympathetic feeling and often an admiration for the person being mirrored. You can often spot the 'intellectual leader' in a group by watching the posture to see who mirrors whom. The practice of mirroring is also developed in salesmen as a tactic for developing a better relationship with customers, particularly at a first meeting.

Contact

Activity

This, like many other aspects of body language, has national associations. The British, for example, are not tactile people, but the French and Belgians are fond of touching and kissing. Degree of touch can indicate intimacy, but it can also be used to re-inforce a strong message. In discussions with people, Margaret Thatcher would often lean forward and take hold of the listener's elbow at a particular point in the conversation where she wanted to make a particular emphasis.

Handshaking is probably the most common form of contact between businessmen. It can give a number of signals. Think, for example, about:

- Who holds his hand out first – and who doesn't hold his hand out, (who is keen to meet and who is not)
- Strength of handshake, (does this indicate strength of personality, particularly in men)
- The angle of the palm, (palm facing down is an indicator of dominance and superiority)
- The double handed handshake, (which is often a cultural habit practised by Americans, or is an attempt to demonstrate particular pleasure at meeting)
- The opportunity to look for nicotine stains, dirty or chewed fingernails, signs of manual labour, (an opportunity seized upon by personnel staff).

Proximity

The distance we stand when talking to people is also culturally determined. In the UK it is acceptable to have a space of about 46cm. Anything less than this can be threatening. In the United States normally, distances are a little greater than this, in the Far East, a little less.

Very often when our space is invaded, such as in a lift or on a London Underground train, we compensate by turning off other non-verbal cues. Thus we look at the floor, or get as far into the corner as we possible can. The last thing we will do is make eye contact.

It is also possible to use proximity to relieve tension in a negotiation. Leaning or moving backwards at times of tension can help to ease the strain. Leaning forward and invading someone's space can be threatening.

Key Learning Point

Orientation

Have you ever felt that someone you are talking to would rather be somewhere else? There are a number of body signals that give this message, facial expressions, gaze and some gestures. The orientation of the body is another one that can give this message. The body often shows where the mind wants to go. Towards the end of a boring conference you may find yourself aiming your body at the door. Sitting in between two people on a settee, you will find your body pointing towards one (and away from the other). You will usually be pointing at the one in whom you have the greatest degree of interest (and giving the 'cold shoulder' to the other).

Try to read something of the two conversations portrayed in Figure 17 below.

Activity

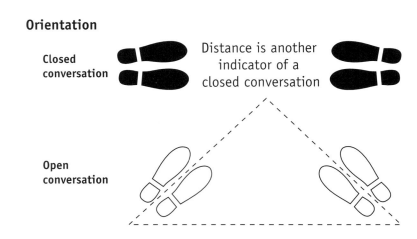

Figure 17

The angle of feet in a conversation between two people, will signal that either the conversation is a closed one (and others are not welcome to join in) or is open and there is an open invitation for someone else to join in. With a closed conversation, the feet tend to point together; in an open conversation it is as though people are standing at two of the three corners of a triangle with an unspoken message to others to come and join in.

Seating arrangements can make use of this point. Seating negotiators opposite each other can encourage direct confrontation. Alternatively a more co-operative setting can be encouraged by setting chairs at right angles across the corner of a table, or by using a round table.

Appearance

The way we dress makes a statement about the values we hold. Dress is the easiest way to send a message about the way that we wish to be seen. The 1980s saw an increase in power dressing and the use of corporate uniforms as young upwardly mobile professionals dressed in pin-stripe suits, with wide brightly coloured braces and gelled hair. There are many other more subtle examples from the man with the old school or regimental tie to the individual who uses a brightly coloured tie to stand out from the crowd.

Even the office dweller who does not enjoy being stereo-typed may feel the need to make a statement with a loud tie emblazoned with a cartoon character.

Some organisations insist upon a dress code as a means of maintaining standards or projecting a corporate image. It is true that it also helps to discourage the non-conformists who are not really welcome.

Summary and concluding remarks

Body language cannot be read like a book. It is as well to treat all non-verbal messages as assumptions and to test them during the negotiation. This can be done quite simply by some form of question such as, 'How do you feel about that?'. If you are to develop skills in reading body language, the negotiator needs to look for clusters of gestures and a lack of congruence between verbal and non-verbal gestures.

It is possible to be mistaken when reading body language, but lack of understanding of the language is more frequently the problem, particularly in areas where gestures are quite similar but have different meanings.

As well as reading non-verbal behaviour, it is important to remember that you should be using body language as part of your negotiating behaviour. It is relatively easy to give the impression that a negotiation is coming to an end by putting your folders into your briefcase, or putting your pen in your pocket, or putting your coat on. You do not have to say you are leaving, but this is clearly the impression you are beginning to create.

Key Learning Point

It is important to remember that there are cultural differences in different parts of the world. Blowing your nose in a negotiation in Japan is considered bad manners and offensive, accepting a business card from a Japanese businessman should be done in a particular way if you are to avoid causing offence. It is important to understand the social context of body language in different countries and cultures.

As a skill it is relatively easy to develop an understanding of body language, and it can pay almost immediate dividends.

Dealing with problems in a negotiation

Chapter 9

What we're saying today is that you're either part of the solution or you're part of the problem.

Eldridge Cleaver

This chapter explains some of the reasons why negotiations start to go wrong. It explains the danger signs to watch for, and explores the actions that can be taken to bring the negotiation back on track. This chapter should be used to diagnose any problems which arise and to prescribe a course of action to deal with them.

What are the problem areas?

Negotiations can start to go wrong for a number of reasons. The other party may have raised something which was not anticipated, they may refuse to move in a key area or quite simply there may be a clash of personalities. Typically, the problems which arise can be summarised under four headings:

Key Learning Point

- Inadequate planning and preparation;

- Poor control;

- Relationship management; or

- Failure to achieve.

The following sections of this chapter explain the symptoms of these problem areas and explain what can be done to resolve any problems that they represent.

Inadequate planning and preparation

Perhaps the most common cause of problems in negotiations is a failure to prepare adequately. There are eight particular aspects of this problem that are frequently encountered which are worthy of discussion:

Failure to identify and develop negotiating strengths and power

There are a number of symptoms of this problem in negotiation. Typically, these include an inability to find a way through the arguments put forward by an opponent, a lack of credible alternative courses of action, and the general realisation that you are in a weak position. Problems may also arise because you are using what power you have in a threatening manner.

It is rarely possible to resolve these problems during a negotiation. Thorough planning and preparation should be used to ensure that:

Action Checklist

- You have made strenuous efforts to identify your strengths and weaknesses and those of the other party;

- You have invested time and resource in identifying and developing your best alternative to a negotiated agreement;

- You have considered alternative forms of power, such as the power of legitimacy, in determining how to deal with your opponent;

- Where you are using power, you are using power to bring people to their senses, rather than to their knees.

Inadequate commitment to specific objectives

A common problem in negotiation is that the negotiator has no clear objectives. Alternatively, the objectives may be set in vague terms, that are not capable of any form of quantification. This means that the negotiation meanders and that the poorly prepared negotiator is particularly susceptible to conditioning by the other party.

The only solution to this problem is to ensure that the negotiator enters the meeting with a range of objectives which include:

Key Learning Point

- An ideal
- A realistic and
- A walk away position.

In co-operative negotiations, it may be sensible to have an exploratory meeting in which there are no specific objectives, but the purpose is to try to define common objectives that both parties are willing to work towards.

Lack of empathy

The problem here is that one negotiator is trying to 'do' the negotiation to the other party, rather than negotiate with the other party. The symptoms of this problem may be confused with the symptoms of failure to identify strengths and power in negotiation. It appears as though your negotiating arguments are having little or no effect on the other party. What is in fact happening is that your arguments fail to resolve problems and issues facing your opponent. In negotiation, the other party is only likely to accept a course of action if it helps to move him further forward.

Stronger attempts need to be made to identify the genuine business interests of the other party, and the key stakeholders within his organisation.

Failure to identify common ground

This is frequently characterised by the negotiation taking an adversarial or confrontational format. The confrontation issues dominate the negotiation, and there is little or no attempt to create a climate in which both sides are willing to work together. This can lead to a spiral in which both sides begin to dig in and defend their respective positions.

To break this spiral, it is important to create the will to work together by emphasising the common ground which exists between both parties, and in effect to play down the problem or disagreement issues. By building these 'bridges of agreement' it is possible to increase the desire for a solution on the part of your opponent.

Key Learning Point

Insufficient consideration to long term issues

This problem is closely associated with the failure to identify and develop common ground. In emphasising common ground, it is also important to emphasise the long term nature of any relationship or potential relationship, and the benefits this could bring, rather than any short term problems which are being resolved.

The research which has been done in this area, suggests that successful negotiators place considerable emphasis on common ground and long term issues, and essentially play down the problem under discussion, whereas the average negotiator builds up the problem, thus making it more difficult to resolve.

Lack of options

The most obvious characteristic of this problem is not knowing how to move the negotiation forward. It stems from either the negotiator having set his objectives too precisely, and thus not having room for manoeuvre, or alternatively, not having considered a wide range of options prior to the face to face meeting.

The negotiator who has identified five or six different ways of resolving a problem is more likely to be successful than the negotiator who only has one way of solving a problem.

To some extent this problem can be overcome by inviting the other party to propose solutions during the negotiation, but there is no real substitute for having made an effort to be creative in the planning phase.

Rigid sequence planning

I was once a spectator at a negotiation where my client had produced an agenda which he tried to stick to rigidly. The problem was that the other party simply refused to discuss the first item on the agenda. My client was unable or unwilling to be flexible and the negotiation stalled on the first item on the agenda.

Another aspect of this problem is when a negotiator has a plan which contains dependencies, that is, it is necessary to discuss one issue before a later issue is discussed. The problem with this approach is very apparent if the other party is unable or unwilling to discuss the first issue until later issues have been discussed.

It is important to avoid rigid sequence planning. The negotiator should be ready and able to deal with each issue independently if necessary.

Insufficient consideration of the mechanics of the negotiation

Negotiations can fail because simple issues have not been given adequate consideration. These issues include the time required to conduct a negotiation, the location in which the negotiation is to take place, those who should be involved in the negotiation have not been, and even the seating arrangements have not been carefully thought through.

All these issues can and should be determined in advance of the negotiation. Some simple solutions are possible:

- If time becomes a pressure in a negotiation, this can be resolved by arranging a subsequent meeting

- In deciding the venue, 'psychological' issues such as home advantage, should be ignored in favour of substantive issues such as:

  - whose information you require access to

  - whether there is benefit to be gained from linking the negotiation to factory visit and

  - practical issues such as the stress and fatigue inducing nature associated with a long motorway drive and the thought of the return trip

  - Seating arrangements can be made which encourage confrontation or co-operation.

Dealing with planning problems

Unfortunately the adverse effects of these planning problems will often be hidden until the face to face meeting takes place. This is when the problems become apparent. Two options exist to help:

1. With major negotiations, there is much to be said for holding a rehearsal in advance. Asking someone to take on the role of the other party will help to form an understanding of the issues they are facing, the questions they are likely to ask, and the answers they are likely to give to your questions.

2. Failing this, the best approach to take when a planning problem becomes apparent in a negotiation, is to ask for recess or to adjourn the meeting until another day. This allows the appropriate amount of re-planning to take place.

Poor control

Once the negotiation is under way, the most commonly encountered problem is lack of control. If the other party take control of the negotiation, they will determine the tone, agenda, pace and direction of the negotiation. Five particular problems are symptomatic of a loss of control. Fortunately they are all relatively easy to deal with. The problem is that it is often difficult to spot them if you are leading the negotiation. It helps if there is someone else in the negotiation on your team who is able to offer advice on how the negotiation process is going.

A poor opening

The most common symptom of a poor opening to negotiation is a speech. In extreme circumstances this may be a long, rambling speech. The net effect of this opening is that the negotiator fails to identify the other party's perspective on the negotiation including his concerns, his view of the issues, and his priorities.

What is required, is a strong opening which galvanises the other party into a positive response. The opening should be short and focused, and include a means of getting the other party's perspective on the issues under discussion. This is best done with a series of non-threatening open questions.

Lack of a common purpose

This is characterised by the negotiation being set up as a confrontation with little or no attempt to secure a common sense of purpose and direction. Most successful negotiations involve both parties working together to resolve common problems.

Key Learning Point

The successful negotiator establishes and maintains a situation where both parties are working together to resolve a set of problems, rather than working against each other. This is best achieved by understanding the other party's position, and demonstrating early in the negotiation that you are seeking to resolve the problems facing both parties rather than just your own.

Inadequate agenda

Many negotiations resemble aimless discussions which lack purpose and direction. During a poorly controlled negotiation there may be times when there appears to be no structure at all. There may be an agenda, but it may be so poorly defined as to allow the negotiation to wander.

Key Learning Point

Civil servants will put considerable effort into defining an agenda in such a way that it provides control and structure for the meeting. In the private sector, we often fail to give adequate consideration to this aspect of negotiation.

A successful negotiator will identify the items that the other party wishes to discuss, and then fashion them into an agenda with his own items. Without being too mechanical, the negotiator then manages to keep the discussion moving in the required direction.

Poor questioning skills

The most apparent sign that one party is in control of the negotiation, is the number of questions being asked. The number of questions being asked by each party, will tell you who is controlling the negotiation.

The successful negotiators establish a sequence of:

- Question,
- Listen,
- Test understanding,
- Move on.

Without the negotiation in any way seeming to be an interrogation, this negotiator gains the information he or she needs and directs the negotiation.

The negotiator will frequently label his behaviour, for example, by saying, 'Can I ask a question?', before asking the question. This behaviour helps to ensure that more questions are answered. It focuses attention on the fact that the next thing that happens requires an answer. It is a particularly useful thing to do if you find that you are having difficulty getting your questions answered. It is a useful behaviour not just with questions, but with proposals, summaries and reactions to proposals.

It is helpful to have a list of key questions prior to the start of the negotiation. These may be questions which get information, questions which seek clarification, questions which test assumptions, and questions which give you time to think. You may also wish to have a number of questions that put the other party firmly under pressure.

Responding to questions inappropriately is also a common way of giving control away. Before answering a question, a negotiator needs to consider whether he will benefit from answering it, rather than simply volunteering an answer. If it is inappropriate to answer it, there are a range of behaviours available, including answering a question with a question, answering a different question, or putting the question on the backburner.

In team negotiations we often suffer from a lack of discipline in answering questions. Two or three people will volunteer an answer, or one person will answer a question and someone else in the team will feel the need to add to the answer. One solution to this problem is to have one person in the team whose role is to act as a 'conduit'. Every time the team is asked a question, the conduit says, 'Before I ask Tom to answer that question, can I just say...' Two things are happening with this behaviour, first of all the conduit is telling the team that Tom, and no-one else, is the man to answer this question, secondly the conduit is giving Tom thirty seconds to think of a good answer.

Key Learning Point

Lack of consolidation of progress

At key points in a negotiation, it is necessary to summarise and move on. By doing this, the successful negotiator makes sure that there is no misunderstanding or disagreement over the salient points.

This is one of those behaviours that everyone agrees with and understands, but many people simply fail to put it into practice. If a negotiation is not going to plan, the easiest way to take control back is to stop, summarise, and ask questions to move back on to the plan.

Relationship management

Relationship management problems are the easiest problems to identify, and often the hardest to resolve. Relationships are like glass; once broken they can never be put together again without the cracks showing. It only takes one moment or one loose word to damage a relationship, and then it can take months of hard work to repair that damage. There are, perhaps, six major problems in this area of negotiation:

Emotional control

We usually negotiate over issues that are important to us. In planning and preparing for a negotiation, we develop views, perspectives and positions that become significant to us. Consequently we become very emotionally attached to the issues. It is, of course, important that we are committed to achieve in the negotiation but this commitment does carry a risk.

It is not uncommon for a negotiator to behave in an emotive and uncontrolled way. In particular, this is likely to take the form of a reaction to the words and behaviours of an opponent. It will often take the form of their loose words or phrases (known as irritators) provoking an escalation. Once emotion takes control of the negotiator, there is a serious risk of the relationship being damaged.

If this happens in a negotiation, the successful negotiator will take control of his emotions. He will not let the words or actions of the opponent cloud his judgement or behaviour. On the contrary, it is important to use emotion in a controlled manner as a method of persuasion and as a way of removing obstacles to progress. Open behaviour, such as an apology, for example, may be an appropriate way of reducing the emotional temperature of the negotiation. It is not necessarily a sign of weakness, but can do much to defuse tension.

Key Learning Point

Sensitivity

Sensitivity problems become apparent when one negotiator is failing to read the signals given by the other party. Anger, defensiveness, frustration, detected at an early stage can be dealt with relatively easily. If these emotions continue unchecked, however, they become much more difficult to deal with.

It is important to continue to listen to what is said, the way things are said, and to heed other messages such as body language, during the negotiation. It is also important to ask the other party at key stages in the negotiation how they feel about particular proposals or suggestions.

If the negotiator fails to be sensitive to what is happening or a problem occurs, some form of positive use of emotion, such as open behaviour may well be appropriate.

Receptivity

It is frustrating in a meeting or a negotiation if others continually refuse to seek your views or even ignore your views on an issue. In a negotiation, if you fail to involve the other party a degree of alienation may occur. The symptoms of this problem are that there is little or no attempt to solicit views or opinions from the other party, and any proposals made by the other party are viewed critically.

To resolve this problem, the negotiator needs to be aware that there are always two parties to the negotiation, both of whom are equally likely to generate problem solving proposals. You should make an active effort to seek views, proposals and opinions from the other party in an attempt to seek a solution, and to keep them involved in the negotiation process.

Even proposals or suggestions that at first seem outlandish should be discussed and if possible enhanced, re-aligned and developed.

Poor use of words

Poor use of words is the most common starting point for relationship problems in a negotiation. One negotiator uses self-centred words rather than invoking a joint approach. Alternatively one negotiator may be patronising or deprecating or mildly offensive in a way which does not invoke an immediate reaction, but gradually builds to the point where the relationship becomes a liability rather than an asset.

To resolve this problem, words and phrases need to be used carefully to ensure that the only emotive response they provoke is positive. Language used should be calculated to generate a shared and positive approach to resolving issues. The term 'we' should be preferred to 'you' or 'I' in the negotiation.

Poor use of body language

Problems may arise if a negotiator's body language is negative or confrontational. Typically this may involve barrier gestures, or confrontation or low response gestures, or threatening gestures. The seating arrangements may cause problems, if negotiators are facing each other directly across the table.

Positive body language can be used to improve the relationship. This may simply involve positive eye contact and smiles, or changing the seating arrangement so that it is across the corner of the table, or adopting gestures that are evaluating rather than disagreeing in meaning.

If tension has set in during a meeting, sitting back and giving the other negotiator more space can relieve the stress.

Lack of a personal dimension to the relationship

Some negotiators seek to exclude all personal feelings and views from a negotiation. This is a mistake. People negotiate, not organisations, and it is important that individuals who are negotiating build a good personal relationship. Problems associated in this area include negotiators who make no attempt to show their feelings, or who adopt low responder models of behaviour. Equally, problems arise if the negotiator does not seek to get his opponents to share their feelings.

If these characteristics are found in a negotiation and it is felt important to resolve them, it is helpful to add a personal dimension to the relationship. This is easily done by giving personal views on issues which are being discussed in the negotiation, and in particular, expressing gratitude, or personal insights into the problems which are being discussed.

Failure to achieve

At the end of the day, planning, control and relationship building are means to an end. That end is to achieve. If you have good control skills and a good relationship with a business partner but fail to achieve, then quite simply, you have failed. There are typically six major problems that arise in relation to achievement. Once these have been overcome, there is a greater chance of success in negotiation.

Poor focus

It is sad to watch a negotiation were one party digresses, rambles and succumbs to argument dilution. This negotiator does not seem to have the ability to keep to the point, or to keep a single objective in sight.

If this is a problem, the negotiator needs to make strenuous efforts to achieve a degree of focus. This must involve having the ability to drag the negotiation back to the issue under discussion. The negotiator must make the effort to avoid being led into digression, irrelevancy, and argument dilution. At no stage in a negotiation should he be distracted from his objective. In many ways, the negotiators must act like the proverbial 'rat down a drain', and be sharply focused on where he is going.

Use of power

Power is central to any negotiation. The two most common problems with power are:

1. The negotiator does not like to use the power he has, for fear of damaging the relationship; or

2. He uses the power in a crude, threatening or offensive way.

It may be necessary to use power in negotiation to achieve a result. It is folly to pretend otherwise. If poor use of power is identified as a problem in negotiation then it is necessary to use power in a way that brings the opponent to his senses, rather than to his knees. This means pointing out the consequences as the course of action that you are trying to avoid, rather than threatening any particular course of action.

Lack of creativity

If the negotiator is too rigid in sticking to the plan, or alternatively sticks to a 'tried and trusted' way of doing things, he may well fail to achieve the required degree of movement from his opponent.

Action Checklist

To a large extent the creative options must be considered during the planning stage and it is too late to begin creative thinking during the face to face stage in the negotiating process. If it is difficult to achieve movement from the opponent, however, it may be necessary to do one of three things:

1. To ask the opponent how he believes the problem should be resolved;

2. To break for a recess and reconsider the options; or

3. To change the package which is being negotiated so that additional variables are available to be used as bargaining chips.

Poorly developed persuasion skills

Most of us have learnt to negotiate through trial and error. Unfortunately, for some of us persuasion is limited to speeches, threats, and repetition of arguments.

If failing to make progress in a negotiation is perceived as a problem, it may be appropriate to consider an alternative technique of persuasion. One computer company trains its sale force to be able to do any negotiation using either logic, power, compromise, trading, emotion or an understanding of the other side's genuine business interests. This gives them the flexibility to be able to make progress any time by switching to an alternative technique of persuasion.

Bad use of time

We frequently fail to make progress in a negotiation because we are making poor use of the time available. Typically, time is wasted early in a negotiation and particularly in the testing phase. This phase of a negotiation can see needless and often endless argument and repetition which does nothing to condition the other party.

If this is a problem in negotiation, the key, particularly in competitive negotiation, is to make sure that all conditioning is effective. Figures and facts should be challenged. Assumptions should be put under great pressure. Argument dilution should be strenuously avoided. If appropriate, the credibility of the opponent's position should be challenged. Stronger use should be made of questions to condition the other party, rather than relying on speeches.

Failure to seize opportunities

Negotiation often takes the form of acceptance or rejection of a series of proposals which are made. This is unfortunate. Every time a number is placed on the negotiating table, it is capable of being stretched. Every time an offer is put on the table, it is capable of being enlarged. To reject these offers is failure to seize opportunities.

Key Learning Point

In a competitive negotiation, every effort should be made to stretch numbers and any large offers. If the other party put a 1% offer on the table, this should not be rejected but stretched, and then additional concessions sought in other areas. Negotiators need to understand that all offers are capable of being stretched, and it is inappropriate to reject offers when they can be enhanced.

Summary and concluding remarks

Not every negotiation will run perfectly, and there is often an inevitability about having to stop to think about what is not going as well as it should and what to do about it. The first thing that is required is a degree of detachment from the negotiation. You need to be able to rise above the negotiation and view the process in such a way that you can see the problem.

This chapter is intended to help you with that process. It is intended to prompt consideration of typical problems and how successful negotiators overcome them. I hope it is helpful.

Summary
checklists

This chapter contains a number of checklists. They summarise many of the key points made throughout the book and are intended to help the reader to understand more about his negotiating style and behaviour and the opportunities which exist for improvement.

Negotiating style

The three sets of questions given below are intended to help you to assess your natural style of negotiation. They are necessarily simple, and you should consider the 'spirit' of your answer, rather than attempting to be too precise. The answers may suggest a need to modify your approach.

Do you find that your negotiations end up in long, protracted arguments?	*If you answered 'yes' to at least three of these questions, you may wish to consider whether your natural negotiating style is too competitive.*
Do you set out in negotiation to satisfy your own objectives, and pay no attention to the needs of the other party?	*In extreme cases, you may achieve in situations where you have a lot of negotiating power, but as part of a long term relationship, you may find that others resent this.*
Do you feel the need to 'get your own back' in negotiation?	
Are you regarded as a very strong and forceful character in negotiation?	*Consider the merits of trying to work with the other party and develop a co-operative style, perhaps based on the Fisher and Ury principles.*
Are you one of these people who always like to win in games and sports?	
Do you hate having arguments with people?	*If you answered 'yes' to at least three of these questions, there is a probability that you are more concerned with the relationship than with achieving.*
Do you find that there are frequently times in negotiation when you have no choice but to compromise?	
Do you feel uncomfortable haggling in a shop?	*You need to consider the legitimacy of your demands and negotiate in a way which makes it clear that you have interests which are paramount.*
Are there some people who you find intimidating?	
Would you prefer not to have to negotiate wherever possible?	*Consider the trading form of negotiation, but insist on equitable trades wherever you can, and do not be afraid to develop a position based on alternatives, but in the negotiation emphasise the fact that you are trying to avoid taking up the alternative courses of action*
Do you believe that there are tactics which always work in negotiation?	*If you have answered 'yes' to at least three of these questions, there is a very real danger that you see negotiation as a Machiavellian exercise.*
Do you look for the sharp angles to use in negotiation?	*There may be a need to seriously consider your view of and approach to negotiation.*
Do you believe it is acceptable in recapping on the negotiation to stress the aspects of the deal which favour you and gloss over those which don't?	*Consider the way that your opponents see you and evaluate the extent to which they will trust you.*
Is negotiation a process which is about gaining the psychological upper hand?	
Do you enjoy one upmanship?	

Planning checklist

This checklist is intended to help you prepare for a negotiation. It concentrates on the process aspects of negotiation:

Have you identified the balance of power?

- Their strengths and weaknesses and yours
- Your BATNA and theirs.

Have you used empathy to understand the other party?

- Their likely objectives
- The questions they are likely to ask you
- The concessions they are likely to want.

Can you identify your genuine interests rather than the negotiating position you are taking?

- Ask yourself why you want something to determine if it is a position or a genuine objective.
- What are their genuine objectives likely to be?
- How can you test your assumptions about their genuine objectives early in the negotiation?
- Is their a creative solution which is likely to satisfy their genuine objectives as well as your own?

Can you identify a strong degree of common ground?

- Is there a history of profitable business for both sides?
- Can you complement them on some aspect of the relationship?
- Can you thank them for some recent actions?

Is a long term aspect to the relationship desirable for both parties?

- Can you change the time frame of the negotiation to emphasise this?
- Can you offer long term benefits?
- Can you undertake joint development initiatives which bring a long term aspect to the relationship?

Is there a radical solution which you could consider?

- In other words, are you constrained by the way things have been done in the past?
- If you didn't have the benefit of experience or custom and practice, what would be the best way to solve the problem?

Are there any benefits to structuring the agenda in a particular way?

- Have you considered all of the issues which the other party will wish to raise?
- Are you capable of dealing with each item on the agenda in a different sequence if you have to do this?

Have you taken into account the 'mechanics' of the negotiation?

- Venue
- Seating
- Who should attend
- Seating arrangements
- Time available.

Competitive negotiation: a checklist of actions

As the negotiation progresses, have you covered all of the following points?

The opening	Introductions	(Authority to negotiate etc.)
	Relationship building	
	Sense of purpose	(Clear understanding and agreement on what you want the negotiation to achieve)
	Control	(Achieved through the agenda and questions)

The testing phase	Challenge assumptions	
	Query facts	
	Point out omissions or inconsistencies	
	Warn of consequences or implications of particular courses of action	
	Do not be afraid to deadlock	(Use the deadlock to apply pressure)
The movement phase	Be gracious with all concessions given – but then ask for more	(No matter how small) (No matter how large)
	Trade concessions - don't give them	
	Use hypothetical links to extract concessions	(If I do this for you, will you do this for me?)
	Adjourn to consider the arithmetic any time you need to	
	If concessions aren't enough, go back to the testing phase and apply more pressure	
The closing phase	Summarise accurately and comprehensively	
	Record and agree the detail	
	Publicise the deal to all interested parties	